THE BRITISH CRIME AND PRISON QUIZ BOOK

JIM DAWKINS AND DAVE COURTNEY

ILLUSTRATED & FOREWORD BY CHARLES BRONSON

APEX PUBLISHING LTD

First published in 2008 by
Apex Publishing Ltd
PO Box 7086, Clacton on Sea, Essex, CO15 5WN

www.apexpublishing.co.uk

Copyright © 2008 by Jim Dawkins and Dave Courtney
The authors have asserted their moral rights

British Library Cataloguing-in-Publication Data
A catalogue record for this book
is available from the British Library

ISBN 1-906358-01-X   978-1-906358-01-3

Typeset in 10.5pt Futura Md BT

Production Manager: Chris Cowlin

Cover Design: Andrew Macey

Illustrations by: Charles Bronson

Printed and bound in Great Britain

FOREWORD

By Charles Bronson

When I was first asked to do this foreword, I thought: this is unusual - The British Crime and Prison Quiz Book! Jim Dawkins and Dave Courtney?! Someone's having a laugh!

But then it hit me: this book is awesome, a complete one off, a masterpiece. And I said to myself: who better to do it than my old pals Jim and Dave? It is brilliant, absolutely magical. Dave an ex-villain and Jim an ex-screw - you just couldn't make up a partnership like that. It's unique - just fantastic; and I'm lucky enough to know both men very well.

I first met Jim in Belmarsh max secure jail on the high risk unit segregation wing. He used to lock me up. To me, he was a true diamond: a man who had a lot of morals and didn't take liberties. He was a 'one-off screw' and all the cons respected him. But, as life goes on, we all move on with it. Jim left the job, walked away from the toe rags, and the rest is history.

All my 'firm' say the same as me: he's a top geezer and we all admire the man. The courage it must have taken to tell the truth about the state of our prison system (in his best-selling, widely acclaimed autobiography, 'The Loose Screw', also published by Apex) is second to none.

Dave... Well, he's just Dave: a complete one-off! A flash git, but a true man of his word. He's stood by me through some serious shit, nothing has ever been too much for him. He is always in my corner and never has a bad word said about me. And he always spoils my mum and sister at the events and shows, and they love him to bits.

I am pleased Dave gave up the crime and moved on to

an honest life. He has published twice as many books as Jeffrey Archer - and *all* Dave's are bestsellers. So who's the daddy?

This book could become a No 1 bestseller purely on the grounds of it being so unusual and unique. I believe it could easily become a collectors item as there is nothing quite like it, nor will there ever be again.

And it will certainly be a winner in our prisons. All 80,000 cons will want one, as will the screws, governors, judges, probation staff, solicitors, and probably even the Old Bill. It might even become a training manual!

This book is also historically accurate, and contains a wealth of information that will both shock and amaze you.

And I will end now by asking my own question...

Can anyone tell me where I buried my loot? I've been locked up for so long that I just can't remember. If anyone can help, get in touch with me at www.freebronson.co.uk or write to me directly at:

Bronson 1314
C.S.C. (cage)
HMP Wakefield
West Yorkshire
WF2 9AG

Yours, in the name of madness,
Charles Bronson

INTRODUCTION
By Jim Dawkins

From its grim beginnings in around 1066, the mysterious world that exists behind our grey prison walls has been a subject that incites great interest.

From the better known images of the Victorian prisons - with their savage regimes and grim punishments - to the romantic images drawn from many near-mythical tales of infamous prisoners, prison life has long been a subject of great fascination. The rich and famous, top politicians and even members of royalty have been seen rubbing shoulders with people linked to the murky underworld of our prison system. Many well-known actresses have been romantically linked to members of the criminal underworld; and many famous actors and members of parliament are known to have spent time in the company of some of our most infamous criminals. And many ex-cons have themselves achieved celebrity status after retiring from their life of crime.

My own interest in our prisons was born in 1992, when - after leaving the army with no qualifications and finding myself in an alien world of mortgages, utility bills and having to pay for food - I entered the employ of HMP as a rather young and slightly naive prison officer.

Actually, I use the word 'interest' rather loosely. At the time, my only interest was in how to survive on the rather grim and frightening landings of Wandsworth prison for long enough to pick up my first pay cheque. I described in my first book and autobiography, 'The Loose Screw' (which details my rather colourful time as a Prison Officer) that stepping inside the grey, imposing walls of Wandsworth prison was like stepping back in time a hundred years.

Nothing had changed from the images I had seen in old Dickensian films and books of old Victorian photographs.

The air was stale. The lingering stench of human waste gave testament to Wandsworth having no integral toilets and prisoners having to 'slop out' using the buckets in their cells. Prisoners all wore the same uniforms (which hadn't changed much since Oscar Wilde's incarceration there): blue and white striped shirts, thin blue denim jeans and black or brown prison shoes. Even in 1992, no prisoner was allowed out of his cell without his shirt's top button done up and his shirt tucked into his trousers. Failure to comply with this rule was an offence that carried sentences ranging from three days solitary confinement to staff "attitude adjustment" sessions. (Those of you with any experience of prison life will understand exactly what I mean by the last statement.)

All together, I spent just over seven years as a Landing Officer in three of London's toughest jails. Two of those were the old Victorian jails (Wandsworth and Wormwood Scrubs), and the third was the new flagship of the prison service, HMP Belmarsh.

During my time as an officer, I became fascinated by the daily routines in the prisons. Many of these routines had been standard for over a hundred years, carried out on the same landings on which I now worked. Prisoners had to endure 'slopping out', weekly showers in the bath house and twenty-three-hour lock-up.

The things I saw in prisons and courtrooms across the country, and the many different characters I met during my career, inspired me to become the first prison officer to document his experiences in an autobiography and, consequently, led to my researching and compiling this quiz book.

I hope you will be amazed by some of the facts you find here, and enjoy testing your knowledge or challenging your friends and family to a quiz night. This book is not biased towards either officer or inmate, and only contains documented facts about our prison system and some of the characters to have passed through it.

All the questions and answers have been thoroughly researched and are genuine facts, including those on the early days of our prison system. Some will test your knowledge of famous (and infamous) prisoners throughout history, literature penned by prisoners and prison-related films and television shows. Others focus on prison facts and figures, including prisoners' entitlements, punishments and prison slang.

So, whether you're a prisoner wanting to test your knowledge of the system in which you find yourself, a prison officer looking to brush-up for a promotion exam, or just a historian with a keen interest in our fascinating penal system: you will find this book invaluable.

I hope you enjoy it!

Jim Dawkins

INTRODUCTION
By Dave Courtney

Hello people. Just like Jim, I've long had an interest in British prisons. As long as I've been getting locked up in them for being a naughty boy, actually. In fact, the last time I saw Jim Dawkins, we were in the category A unit at HMP Belmarsh and he was hitting me over the head with a truncheon ... Just kidding!

Seriously though, if you'd told me a few years ago that I'd be writing books with an ex-screw, I would have had you sectioned. But I got to tell you, Jim is no ordinary ex-screw.

Anyone who knows me will tell you I won't work with any old muppet. I've always had a healthy respect for the military, and like to run my own affairs with that discipline and respect I describe in all my books (and Jim describes in his first book, 'The Loose Screw'). Jim and I both learned to work this way while growing up on the streets of South London; a lesson that has served us both well, it would seem, in our two very different career paths.

I first met Jim when he was one of the screws on the Cat A unit in Belmarsh, and - although he was then The Enemy - I remember noticing he was somehow different to the rest. Don't get me wrong - he was no pushover; he just seemed to be fair and unbothered about upsetting his colleagues as long as he did his job professionally. This strength of character quickly earned him the healthy respect of many of the chaps doing bird at that time.

Our paths crossed again in early 2000 when Jim asked me for some help with a book he was writing, 'The Loose Screw'. The book exposed the unprofessional behaviour of certain screws that all ex-prisoners could confirm, but that had, until Jim's book, been kept by the prison officers a closely guarded secret. We seemed to hit it off and - whilst Jim may not agree with some of my outlook on life, and I may not agree with some of his - we quickly formed a good partnership.

These days, I prefer to spend my time educating youngsters in the pitfalls of being involved in crime and wasting their lives in prison. With Jim on my team, we provide a valuable insight from both sides of the fence.

When I was asked to co-author this book, I jumped at the chance. Jim and I have worked very hard to compile a interesting variety of historical facts. Some are extremely serious and some are pretty funny, but all are 100% accurate. Our aim was to please a varied audience: guys trying to pass the time while doing a bit of bird, prison officers looking for promotion and maybe even judges looking for guidance in court. We have also compiled a more comprehensive answer section in order to give the reader an informative read, rather than just yes or no answers.

As you can see by the cover, I'm the good looking one in our partnership, but I think we both have something worthwhile to say. By the end of this, I hope those of you who don't know either myself or Jim - or began with the opinion that we are just an uneducated ex-criminal and an ex-screw - will see that we have good heads on our shoulders and a genuine mission to prevent young people becoming involved in lives of crime.

I hope you enjoy the challenges in this book and I hope one day to meet you, perhaps at one of our future venues.

Dave Courtney

CONTENTS

THE EARLY DAYS OF CRIME AND PUNISHMENT

Q1: Who introduced the first formal legal system in Britain?
a: The Celts
b: The Normans
c: The Romans
d: The Saxons

Q2: What was the main method of catching lawbreakers during the Middle Ages?
a: Hue and Cry
b: Shout and Scream
c: Jeer and Snigger
d: Point and Stare

Q3: Up until the twentieth century, the Tower of London was used as a prison for important prisoners. Who built it?
a: Queen Victoria
b: Charles II
c: Henry VIII
d: William the Conqueror

Q4: What was Traitors' Gate originally called?
a: The Tower Gate
b: The River Gate
c: The Water Gate
d: The Salt Gate

Q5: How many queens of England were executed at The Tower of London?
a: 0
b: 3
c: 5
d: 7

Q6: Ludgate Prison was situated near which famous London landmark?
a: Trafalgar Square
b: St Pauls Cathedral
c: Buckingham Palace
d: Houses of Parliament

Q7: Which of the following held prisoners in Norman times and continued to do so until the twentieth century?
a: Milbank
b: Ludgate
c: Newgate
d: The Clink

Q8: Who first ordered the building of the jails in every county?
a: Elizabeth I
b: Henry II
c: Charles II
d: Henry VIII

Q9: In 1423, Dick Whittington was the Mayor of London and was so concerned about the state of his city's prisons that he ordered one of them to be rebuilt. The prison was subsequently named after him. Which prison was it?
a: Whittington's Ludgate?
b: Whittington's State Penitentiary?
c: Whittington's Newgate?
d: Whittington's Milbank

Q10: True or false: In addition to the main prisons in our cities, there were also a number of smaller privately-run prisons known as 'Compters'?

Q11: London's first prison to be designed and built from scratch as a state prison stood on the banks of a well-known London river from Norman times right through to the Victorian era. What was its name?
a: The Seine
b: The Brent
c: The Fleet
d: The Thames

Q12: 'Execution Dock', where British pirates were hung, was located on the banks of the Thames at which location?
a: Greenwich
b: Deptford
c: Embankment
d: Wapping

Q13: Where is London's smallest gaol?
   a: Horsemonger Lane gaol
   b: Pudding Lane Compter
   c: The Houses of Parliament
   d: Brixton

Q14:   What have Jeremy Bentham, John Howard and Elizabeth Fry got in common?
   a: They were all hanged at Newgate
   b: They were all prison governors
   c: They were all involved with the Gordon rioters
   d: They were all concerned with prison reform

Q15:   What names were the ships used to transport prisoners to Australia given after being converted into floating prisons?
   a: Liners
   b: Hulks
   c: Floats
   d: They were never converted for use as floating prisons

Q16:   What is London's oldest gaol that still accepts prisoners today?
   a: Wandsworth
   b: Brixton
   c: Wormwood Scrubs
   d: Pentonville

Q17:   Milbank Prison opened in 1816 and became a huge success because it demonstrated new ideas and theories on the structure of prisons. True or false?

Q18: Which prison was historically used to house religious prisoners?
a: Ludgate
b: The Clink
c: The Fleet
d: Holloway

Q19: Which London prison became known as 'The portal to the penal colonies'?
a: The Fleet
b: Pentonville
c: Newgate
d: Wandsworth

Q20: During what period did Britain transport criminals to Australia, and how many prisoners do official records state were sent there?
a: Between 1787 and 1868, around 164,000 people were transported to Australia.
b: Between 1797 and 1878, around 140,000 people were transported to Australia.
c: Between 1777 and 1858, around 120,000 people were transported to Australia.
d: Between 1767 and 1848, around 100,000 people were transported to Australia.

Q21: Before Britain began transporting its convicts to Australia, prisoners were sent to another penal colony. Where was this situated?
a: Devil's Island
b: North America
c: The Caribbean
d: North Africa

Q22: What was the name of the first 'convict ship' sent to Australia with a cargo of entirely female and child prisoners?
a: Lady Penrhyn
b: Lady Juliana
c: Neptune
d: Guardian

Q23: By what name is London's 'Central Criminal Court' better known?
a: The Royal Courts of Justice
b: Middlesex Guildhall Law Court
c: The Old Bailey
d: Inner London Law Courts

Q24: True or false: The Court of Appeal is the most senior court in the English legal system?

Q25: What is the title of the most senior permanent Judge of the Central Criminal Court?
a: The Recorder of London
b: Common Sergeant of London
c: The Recorder
d: His Lordship of London

Q26: What disease became known as 'gaol fever' and, at one time, claimed more lives in our prisons than the hangman's noose?
a: Typhoid
b: Cholera
c: Typhus
d: Smallpox

Q27: Mount Pleasant Postal Sorting Office stands on the
site of a once notorious London Jail. What was its
name?
a: Newgate
b: Clerkenwell
c: Ludgate
d: Millbank

Q28: By what name was Clerkenwell Prison known when
first built (during the reign of King James I)?
a: Coldbath Fields Prison
b: Coldblow Lane Prison
c: Coldharbour Prison
d: Coldwind Blow Prison

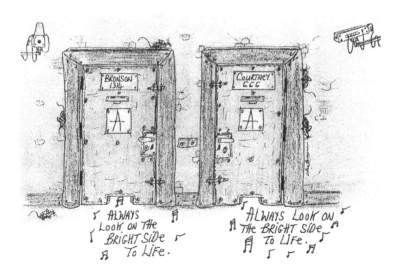

LITERATURE IN PRISON

Q29: Which prison was John Bunyon held in when he wrote 'Pilgrims Progress'?
a: Millbank
b: Newgate
c: Bedford
d: York

Q30: Which jail was Oscar Wilde sent to after his conviction for gross indecency?
a: The Clink
b: Marshalsea
c: Ludgate
d: Reading

Q31: Complete the name of the well-known 19th century literary publication: 'The Prisoner of...'
a: Zenda
b: The Legion
c: The Ayottolah
d: Azkaban

Q32: While in prison, Oscar Wilde wrote an essay addressed to his former friend, Lord Alfred Douglas, that is generally described as an 'apologia' for his way of life. Its title is taken from the opening of which of the Psalms in Latin?
a: Beatus vir
b: Dixit Dominus
c: Miserere
d: De profundis

Q33: One of the leading philosophers of the twentieth century fought in the Austro-Hungarian army during World War I. He wrote part of his principal work, the 'Tractatus Logico-Philosophicus' while being held as a prisoner of war in Italy. Who was he?
a: Martin Buber
b: Rudolf Steiner
c: Karl Popper
d: Ludwig Wittgenstein

Q34: John Cleland, imprisoned for debt 1748–49, wrote a novel called 'Memoirs of a Woman of Pleasure'. It is said to have made £10,000 (over £1 million in 2006 terms) for his publisher, but only twenty guineas for him. During the next two centuries, many people were imprisoned for publishing and/or selling the novel. Today, the work is generally known by the name of its heroine - what is this?
a: Clarissa
b: Moll Flanders
c: Fanny Hill
d: Pamela

Q35: In 1792, an English radical - fleeing from arrest for seditious libel in England - was warmly welcomed in revolutionary France. Before long, however, his popularity waned; and he spent nearly a year in prison, where he wrote Part 2 of his work 'The Age of Reason' Who was he?
a: William Hone
b: Thomas Paine
c: William Blake
d: William Godwin

Q36: Which English cavalier poet wrote 'To Althea, from Prison', with the opening couplet: "Stone walls do not a prison make, nor iron bars a cage"?
a: Thomas Carew
b: Robert Herrick
c: John Suckling
d: Richard Lovelace

Q37: The 'Morte d'Arthur', a 15th century collection of Arthurian legends, is believed to have been compiled in prison. What was the name of the author?
a: William Langland
b: William Caxton
c: Thomas Malory
d: Geoffrey Chaucer

Q38: Daniel Defoe was a 17th century English writer, journalist and spy who was imprisoned in Newgate jail. What is his most famous novel?
a: Swallows and Amazons
b: Robinson Crusoe
c: My Fair Lady
d: Nell Gwynn

Q39: The faithful servant of King Henry VIII became Lord Chancellor in 1529; but, in the 1530s, refused to recognise the King as head of the English church and was consequently imprisoned and beheaded for treason. While in prison he wrote 'A Dialogue of Comfort Against Tribulation'. Who was he?
a: Thomas Cranmer
b: Thomas Wolsey
c: Thomas Cromwell
d: Thomas More

Q40: Which famous English explorer, soldier, courtier and poet wrote 'A History of the World' while imprisoned in the Tower of London for alleged treason against James VI and I?
a: Robert Devereux, Earl of Essex
b: Sir Thomas Wyatt
c: Sir Francis Drake
d: Sir Walter Raleigh

Q41: Which Dickens novel features the Central Criminal Court?
a: A Tale of Two Cities
b: Little Dorit
c: Oliver Twist
d: Hard Times

Q42: In which year did John Howard review British prisons and publish his novel 'The State of The Prisons'?
a: 1677
b: 1777
c: 1877
d: 1977

Q43: A well-known English journalist, famously credited with creating the interview technique, spent time in two London jails before his death on the Titanic. Who was he?
a: William Thomas Stead
b: Thomas William Stead
c: Jack Dawson
d: Lawrence Beesley

Q44: Adolf Hitler wrote his memoirs, 'Mein Kampf', whilst serving a sentence in which prison?
a: Spandau Prison
b: Landsberg Prison
c: Stammheim Prison
d: Werl Prison

Q45: David McMillan wrote an autobiographical account of his imprisonment and 1996 escape from which notorious prison?
a: Klong Prem Prison
b: Devil's Island
c: Changi Prison
d: Robben Island

Q46: Name the identical twin sisters who were the subject of Marjorie Wallace's book, 'The Silent Twins', authored several novels (including 'The Pepsi Cola Addict' and 'The Pugilist') and who spent fourteen years in Broadmoor.
a: June and Jennifer Gibbons
b: Jade and Jennifer Gibbons
c: Jane and Jennifer Gibbons
d: June and Jessica Gibbons

HISTORICAL FIGURES IN PRISON

Q47: In which tower was Sir Walter Raleigh held prisoner for 13 years?
a: St Thomas's Tower
b: The Bloody Tower
c: The Martin Tower
d: The White Tower

Q48: A famous queen was imprisoned in Staffordshire for a period of time. Who was she?
a: Queen Elizabeth I
b: Mary Queen of Scots
c: Queen Anne Boleyn
d: Queen Anne

Q49: Which Lord Chancellor was found guilty of corruption in the early 18th century?
a: Thomas Parker
b: Norman Parker
c: Jack Straw
d: Lord Harcourt

Q50: In which prison did Charles Dickens' father serve time for debt?
a: Newgate
b: The Clink
c: The Marshalsea
d: Rochester

Q51: William Kidd (aka Captain Kidd, the infamous pirate-hunter-turned-pirate) was held in which notorious London prison prior to his execution?
a: Newgate
b: The Fleet
c: Millbank
d: Ludgate

Q52: Where was Guy Fawkes imprisoned and interrogated, before being hung drawn and quartered for masterminding the gunpowder plot?
a: Newgate
b: Tower of London
c: Highgate
d: Tyburn

Q53: 'The Man in The Iron Mask' languished in a prison in what part of the world?
a: Britain
b: France
c: Beirut
d: America

Q54: Who was the youngest convict to be transported to Australia?
a: Mary Wade
b: Elizabeth Steele
c: Kylie Tennant
d: Mary Frith

Q55: Who was reportedly the UK's first 'bent' policeman, and perhaps the most famous 18th century criminal in the country?
a: Oscar Wild
b: Jack Wild
c: Jonathan Wild
d: Arthur Wild

Q56: Jack Sheppard is Newgate jail's most famous escapologist. How many times did he successfully escape from the notorious London jail?
a: 1
b: 2
c: 3
d: 4

Q57: The Central Criminal Court in London was originally intended to handle trials of only those crimes committed in the capital city. This changed in 1856 when a Staffordshire doctor was allowed to stand trial here, due to concerns about his not getting a fair trial in his native Stafford. Who was he and what were the nature of his offences?
a: William Palmer, a poisoner and murderer
b: Jack Palmer, a rapists and murderer
c: Robert Palmer, a philanthropist
d: Daniel Palmer, a body snatcher and human organ seller

Q58: Who was the Scotsman convicted of high treason after an assassination attempt on Queen Victoria at Windsor, who escaped the noose in 1882?
a: Roderick McLean
b: Robert McLean
c: Rupert McLean
d: Richard McLean

Q59: Who was the first person to be convicted on fingerprint evidence in the United Kingdom?
a: Harry Jackson
b: Colin Jackson
c: Albert Jackson
d: Henry Jackson

Q60: Which famous doctor spent time in Pentonville before his execution for the murder of his wife on January 31 1910?
a: Dr Crippen
b: Dr Jekyll
c: Dr Shipman
d: Dr Bodkin Adams

Q61: Rudolf Hess was imprisoned in which London prison?
a: The Tower of London
b: Wormwood Scrubs
c: Brixton
d: Pentonville

Q62: Where and when did the infamous nazi deputy, Rudolf Hess, die?
a: The Tower of London
b: Spandau Prison
c: At home, in Dresden Germany
d: Berlin Military Hospital

Q63: Lord Haw Haw, the traitor behind the German propaganda broadcasts during WWII, was better known by what name?
a: William Wallace
b: William Joyce
c: William Kraus
d: William Boyce

Q64: Where was Lord Haw Haw held - and eventually executed - for three counts of high treason after his capture at the end of the war?
a: Wandsworth
b: Pentonville
c: Wormwood Scrubs
d: Latchmere House

Q65: Who was the only British soldier to be executed for treachery during WWII, and the last man to be hung in Britain for a crime other than murder?
a: William Joyce
b: John Amery
c: Theodore Schurch
d: David Stirling

Q66: Who was the infamous, British MI6-agent-turned-KGB-spy imprisoned in 1961 on three counts of treason?
a: John Amery
b: William Joyce
c: George Blake
d: Boris Jensen

Q67: The actions of the spy detailed in Q66 so outraged the government that he was given the   longest prison sentence ever decided by a British Court at that time. How many years was he sentenced to?
a: 35
b: 42
c: 53
d: 90

Q68: In which prison was the spy detailed in Q66 held after his conviction and did he subsequently escape from in 1966?
a: Wormwood Scrubs
b: Latchmere House
c: Pentonville
d: Wandsworth

Q69: The escape of the KGB spy in 1966 was rumoured to have been orchestrated by which organisation(s)?
a: The KGB
b: The IRA
c: Al Qaeda
d: The KGB, IRA and the British Security Services

Q70: Who was given the name 'Houdini' after his famous escape from Nottingham Prison in the mid 1950s and two subsequent escapes from other high security establishments?
a: Alfie Watts
b: Alfie Moon
c: Alfie Hinds
d: Alfie Harris

Q71: Who was the subject of a countrywide campaign to secure his appeal against a twenty-year sentence for armed robbery in 1975? (His name could be seen on almost every railway bridge in London at the time as graffiti protesting his innocence.)
a: George Davies
b: George Dawson
c: George Dark
d: George Dawes

Q72: Who was the first man to be convicted of a murder committed on a British train?
a: Thomas Briggs
b: Franz Muller
c: Jonathen Wild
d: Daniel Williamson

THE VICTORIAN ERA

Q73: Of the six, large London prisons in use today, which four were built in the Victorian era?
a: Wormwood Scrubs, Belmarsh, Pentonville and Holloway
b: Brixton, Milbank, Wandsworth and Wormwood Scrubs
c: Wormwood Scrubs, Milbank, Pentonville and Brixton
d: Wandsworth, Wormwood Scrubs, Pentonville and Brixton

Q74: Who built Wormwood Scrubs?
a: Irish Labourers
b: Ex-Servicemen
c: Local contractors
d: Prisoners

Q75: From 1906, Holloway began receiving a particularly difficult group of prisoners. Who were they?
a: Female members of the Gordon rioters
b: Female members of the IRA
c: Suffragettes
d: Nurses captured in Africa during the Boer Wars

Q76: What was established in 1850 that gave our prisons a structure similar to the one we know today?
a: The Penal Society
b: The Prison Service
c: The John Howard Prisons Society
d: The Convict Service

Q77: In what year was the Prisons Act passed?
a: 1868
b: 1858
c: 1878
d: 1848

Q78: True or false: Wandsworth Prison, opened in 1851, was revolutionary in that each cell had a working toilet (which most homes did not at the time).

Q79: What was HMP Wandsworth's name when it was first opened?
a: HMP Wandsworth
b: The Wandsworth Correctional Facility
c: The Earlsfield Centre of Penal Reform
d: The Surrey House of Correction

Q80: Dartmoor Prison was originally built to house prisoners from which war?
a: The Crimean War
b: The Napoleonic War
c: The American War
d: The Zulu wars

Q81: On 6 April 1815, an apparently drunk British officer prematurely gave the order to open fire on a group of inmates, causing a commotion and killing seven. What nationality were the inmates who were killed?
a: French
b: Russian
c: American
d: Boers

Q82: In what year was Strangeways prison first built?
a: 1866
b: 1867
c: 1868
d: 1869

Q83: Which prison was Strangeways built to replace?
a: Newgate Prison
b: Millbank Prison
c: New Bailey Prison
d: Salford Prison

Q84: Sir Evelyn Ruggles-Brise, a prison commissioner, introduced the system that separated youths from adult men in the prison system. In what year was the first institution for boys established?
a: 1898
b: 1900
c: 1902
d: 1908

Q85: Near which town was the first institution for youth prisoners established?
a: Feltham
b: Portland
c: Rochester
d: Dover

Q86: The Prison Act of 1865 was brought about to make prison life even tougher for prisoners. What rules were introduced to make the regime more miserable?
a: The removal of sanitation, and reinstatement of 'slop out' buckets for waste
b: The 'silent system'
c: Hard bed, board and labour
d: Bread and Water

Q87: In 1877, control of our prisons was handed over to the Home Office. What was the normal sentence handed out at this time?
a: One year in solitary, followed by three years hard labour.
b: One year in solitary, followed by two years hard labour.
c: Two years in solitary, followed by one years hard labour.
d: Three years in solitary, followed by three years hard labour.

Q88: Victorian prisons were run on both the 'separate' and 'silent' systems. Which American prison had the regime that the 'separate system' was based on?
a: Alcatraz
b: Cherry Hill
c: Sing Sing
d: Auburn

Q89: Which prison opened in 1842 with the new 'separate system'?
a: Wandsworth
b: Newgate
c: Brixton
d: Pentonville

Q90: Which American prison had the regime that the 'silent system' was based on?
a: Auburn
b: Sing Sing
c: Cherry Hill
d: Alcatraz

Q91: One form of monotonous 'work' in the silent system was known as 'picking oakum'. What did this refer to?
a: Unstitching mail bags
b: Unstitching damaged ships' sails for repair
c: Separating old bits of rope strands
d: Picking woodworm out of wood for furniture making

EXECUTIONS IN PRISON

Q92: There are four official methods of judicial hanging. What are they?
a: Suspension hanging, short drop, standard drop and long drop
b: Suspension drop, short drop, standard drop and long drop
c: Suspension hanging, short drop, standard hanging and long drop
d: Suspension hanging, shock drop, standard drop and long drop

Q93: How many prisoners were executed at the Tower of London?
a: 7
b: 70
c: 53
d: 19

Q94: Where was the principle site of execution between 1177 and 1783?
a: Newgate
b: Tyburn
c: Traitors Gate
d: Highgate

Q95: After the abolition of public executions in 1868, which prison housed the first 'execution shed' in one of its exercise yards?
a: Wandsworth
b: Pentonville
c: Brixton
d: Wormwood Scrubs

Q96: Where and when was Britain's last ever double hanging?
a: Pentonville, June 17 1954
b: Wansdworth, July 17 1955
c: Strangeways, January 17 1953
d: Brixton, June 17 1955

Q97: When were double hangings finally outlawed, and which act was this decreed by?
a: The Homicide Act of 1954.
b: The Executions Act of 1955.
c: The Hanging Act of 1953.
d: The Homicide Act of 1957.

Q98: How many condemned prisoners were hanged in Pentonville between 1902 and 1961?
a: 70
b: 120
c: 210
d: 170

Q99: Who was the youngest woman to die judicially under English law in the twentieth century?
a: Ruth Ellis
b: Irma Grese
c: Juana Bormann
d: Elisabeth Volkenrath

Q100: In what year was Derek Bentley (the young man with the mental age of eleven) hung for the murder of a policeman?
a: 1952
b: 1953
c: 1954
d: 1955

Q101: Where was Bentley executed?
a: Wandsworth
b: Pentonville
c: Wormwood Scrubs
d: Brixton

Q102: After his death, Bentley's sister, Iris, led a tireless campaign to clear his name. In what year did she finally win her battle?
a: 1993
b: 1995
c: 1998:
d: 2006

Q103: Ruth Ellis, hanged for the murder of her lover, was the last woman to be executed. Name her lover.
a: David Blakely
b: David Bentley
c: David Barker
d: David Barton

Q104: Where and when was Ruth Ellis executed?
a: Pentonville in July 1955
b: Holloway in July 1956
c: Wandsworth in July 1956
d: Holloway in July 1955

Q105: Name the well-known British hangman:
a: Albert Pierrepoint
b: John Ellis
c: Alfred Allen
d: William Billington

Q106: How many prisoners were executed by Albert Pierrepoint?
a: 429
b: 435
c: 395
d: 433

Q107: How many *female* prisoners were executed by Albert Pierrepoint?
a: 7
b: 12
c: 17
d: 22

Q108: How many prisoners were executed in Wandsworth between 1878 and 1961?
a: 165
b: 225
c: 135
d: 195

Q109: Where were the country's last working hanging cell and gallows situated until they were dismantled in 1998?
a: HMP Belmarsh
b: HMP Hull
c: HMP Wandsworth
d: HMP Brixton

Q110: Which charge is the only one left in English law to carry the death penalty?
a: Terrorism
b: Theft against the Crown
c: Treason against the Crown
d: Threats against the Crown

Q111: Which two prisons were the last to hang prisoners on the same day?
a: HMP Walton and HMP Strangeways
b: HMP Wandsworth and HMP Holloway
c: HMP Wandsworth and HMP Pentonville
d: HMP Wormwood Scrubs and HMP Wandsworth

Q112: Name the hangmen responsible for carrying out the executions detailed in Q111?
a: Albert Pierrepoint and John Ellis
b: Harry Allen and Robert Leslie Stewart
c: Alfred Allen and William Billington
d: William Billington and John Ellis

Q113: Who was hung for the notorious 'A6 Murder' in 1961, and the eighth-to-last person to be hung for murder in Britain?
a: William Hanratty
b: Jonathan Hanratty
c: James Hanratty
d: Raymond Hanratty

FAMOUS AND INFAMOUS PRISONERS AND THEIR ASSOCIATES

Q114: From which prison did Ronnie Biggs escape while at the start of his thirty-year sentence for a minor part in 'the Great Train Robbery'?
a: Brixton
b: Wandsworth
c: Belmarsh
d: Wormwood Scrubs

Q115: Name the only three prisoners ever to have dared walk across the hallowed, brass, octagonal-shaped grille that makes up Wandsworth's famous centre.
a: Ronnie Biggs, Charlie Bronson and Dave Courtney
b: Ronnie Kray, Reggie Kray and Frank Fraser
c: Frank Fraser, Frank "the Mad Axeman" Mitchell and Roy "Pretty Boy" Shaw
d: Frank 'the Mad Axeman' Mitchell, Charlie Bronson and Frank Fraser

Q116: On how many occasions did Charlie Bronson defy staff at Wandsworth and walk over the highly polished brass grille at the centre of the prison?
a: 1
b: 2
c: 3
d: 4

Q117: Who was the famous London gangster who - before the Kray Twins - ran various protection rackets in the East End of London, and received jail sentences for various offences (including armed robbery)?
a: Billy Hill
b: Jimmy Hill
c: Benny Hill
d: Johnny Hill

Q118: Jack Spot was a London gangster of Jewish origin, with links to most of the protection rackets of his time. But for what is he most famous?
a: The downfall of the Kray twins
b: The disappearance of Frank Mitchell
c: His involvement in the Cable Street Riots
d: His being ringleader of the Wormwood Scrubs riots

Q119: What did Charlie Bronson do after he ran across Wandsworth's brass grille?
a: Chinned the centre PO
b: Locked himself in the centre office
c: Rang the brass bell located near the office
d: Took the centre PO hostage and locked himself and the PO in the centre office

Q120: Charlie Bronson set a new world record for continuous medicine ball sit-ups, in Belmarsh segregation unit exercise yard. How many did he complete in one hour?
a: 1,790
b: 1,890
c: 1,990
d: 2,090

Q121: Who famously 'chinned' the well-known hangman, Albert Pierrepoint, in Wandsworth Prison?
a: Roy Shaw
b: Charlie Bronson
c: Frank Fraser
d: Lenny MacLean

Q122: Who escaped with John McVicar from Durham Special Unit?
a: Wally Probyn
b: Ronnie Biggs
c: Frank Mitchell
d: Frank Frazer

Q123: On which prison's roof has Charlie Bronson carried out three separate rooftop protests?
a: Parkhurst
b: Wandsworth
c: Hull
d: Broadmoor

Q124: How many years did 'Mad Frank Fraser' spend in jail?
a: 39
b: 40
c: 41
d: 42

Q125: During his time in the prison system, how many times was Frank Fraser certified insane?
a: 1
b: 2
c: 3
d: 4

Q126: In how many prisons has Roy "Pretty Boy" Shaw been incarcerated?
a: 6
b: 18
c: 12
d: 22

Q127: What did Dave Courtney wear for his appearance before Bow Street Magistrates Court on a charge of perverting the course of justice?
a: A dinner jacket
b: A Borat swimsuit
c: A basque
d: A court jesters outfit

Q128: Name the only two prisoners to have escaped from a prison exercise yard using a helicopter.
a: Sid Draper and John Kendall
b: Eric Mason and Ronnie Field
c: 'Dingus' McGee and John Cunningham
d: John McFadden and Tony Bolden

Q129: Ronnie Kray was certified insane twice. Name the two prisons in which he was being held at those times and the decades in which he was certified.
a: Wandsworth and Parkhurst; 50s and 60s.
b: Maidstone and Winchester; 60s and 70s.
c: Wandsworth and Winchester; 50s and 70s.
d: Winchester and Parkhurst; 50s and 70s.

Q130: Who did Reggie Kray marry whilst he was in Maidstone Prison?
a: Francis
b: Roberta
c: Kate
d: Emily

Q131: Name three of 'the Great Train Robbers'.
a: Bruce Reynolds, Charlie Wilson and Ronnie Biggs.
b: Ronnie Biggs, Charlie Richardson and Kenneth Noye.
c: Richard Wilson, Charlie Kray and 'Buster' Edwards.
d: Bruce Reynolds, Ronnie Biggs and Charlie Breaker.

Q132: Who investigated 'the Great Train Robbery' of 1963?
a: John Stalker
b: Jack Sweeney
c: Leonard Reed
d: Jack Slipper

Q133: Name the two inmates charged with being the ringleaders of the Strangeways riots.
a: Charlie McGee and Jason Mitchell
b: Paul Lord and Allen Taylor
c: Paul Taylor and Andy Lord
d: Allen Lord and Paul Taylor

Q134: Name the only ex-criminal to officially stand for London Mayor.
a: Charlie Bronson
b: Frankie Fraser
c: Charlie Richardson
d: Dave Courtney

Q135: Who pulled off the £60million Knightsbridge safety deposit box raid, much to the embarrassment of the authorities?
a: Valerio Viccei
b: Mickey McEvoy
c: Roy Shaw
d: Freddie Foreman

Q136: Who was the infamous convicted poisoner who died in custody in Parkhurst in the 90s?
a: Graham Young
b: Graham West
c: Graham Crest
d: Graham North

Q137: Who has been convicted of killing three other inmates while he has been in prison?
a: Bob Winters
b: Bob Saunders
c: Bob Maudsley
d: Bob Walmer

Q138: Charlie Bronson took part in England's longest ever prison siege. In which prison did it take place?
a: Broadmoor
b: Wakefield
c: Hull
d: Parkhurst

Q139: In which prison was Charlie Bronson stabbed over a dozen times in the back by fellow prisoners - an attack that he survived.
a: Parkhurst
b: Wakefield
c: Wormwood Scrubs
d: Full Sutton

Q140: In which prison did Charlie Bronson famously take the Iraqi Stanstead airport hijackers hostage?
a: Belmarsh
b: Full Sutton
c: Hull
d: Long Lartin

Q141: Name two of 'the Birmingham Six'.
a: Hugh Callaghan and Paddy Hill
b: Gerard Hunter and Richard McIlkenny
c: William Power and John Walker
d: William Walker and Richard Callaghan

Q142: Who was Charlie Bronson's unlicensed fight promoter and manager?
a: Noel Edmunds
b: Frank Warren
c: Jimmy Tibbs
d: Paul Edmunds

Q143: Name this country's first ever 'supergrass'.
a: Bertie Big
b: Bertie Smalls
c: Charlie Large
d: Harry Huge

Q144: Who was dubbed 'the Nail Bomber'?
a: Andy Copeland
b: Paddy Copeland
c: Jimmy Copeland
d: David Copeland

Q145: Name the prisoner who maimed Peter Sutcliffe by stabbing him in the eye with a biro in Broadmoor special hospital.
a: Danny Kay
b: Peter Kay
c: Ian Kay
d: Jason Kay

Q146: Which well-known ex-prisoner and bestselling author has the nickname 'Pretty Boy'?
a: Dave Courtney
b: Frank Fraser
c: Roy Shaw
d: Howard Marks

Q147: Who was once known as 'the Yellow Pages of the Underworld'?
a: Freddie Foreman
b: Lennie McLean
c: Joe Pyle
d: Dave Courtney

Q148: Which hugely successful, bestselling author spent a long time in prison and is known as 'Mr Nice'?
a: Charlie Bronson
b: Howard Marks
c: Norman Parker
d: Mark 'Chopper' Reid

Q149: The Prison-Officer-turned-bestselling-author, Jim Dawkins, served in three of London's toughest jails. Which prisons were they?
a: Belmarsh, Pentonville and Wandsworth
b: Brixton, Wormwood Scrubs and Wandsworth
c: Wormwood Scrubs, Belmarsh and Holloway
d: Belmarsh, Wandsworth and Wormwood Scrubs

Q150: Which former 'Mr Strongman' contestant was a gym Prison Officer at Wandsworth Prison for many years?
a: Gary Taylor
b: Geoff Capes
c: Jamie Reeves
d: Terry Hollands

Q151: Who was known as 'the Mad Axeman'?
a: Frank Mitchell
b: Reggie Kray
c: Frankie Fraser
d: Ronnie Kray

Q152: Which prison did the Kray twins famously arrange Frank Mitchell's' escape from?
a: Wandsworth
b: Durham
c: Dartmoor
d: Frankland

Q153: Where did Kate Kray marry Ronnie Kray?
a: Parkhurst
b: Maidstone
c: Broadmoor
d: Rampton

Q154: Which well-known underworld figure had his leg broken in the 1969 Parkhurst riots, and was later charged with being a ringleader?
a: Eric Mason
b: Reggie Kray
c: Frankie Fraser
d: Charlie Richardson

Q155: Can you name the six prisons of which Charlie Bronson has managed to get on to the roof?
a: Parkhurst, Hull, Leicester, Winchester, Wandsworth and Broadmoor.
b: Wakefield, Hull, Leicester, Winchester, Wandsworth and Broadmoor.
c: Parkhurst, Hull, Leicester, Wakefield, Wandsworth and Broadmoor.
d: Parkhurst, Hull, Leicester, Winchester, Woodhill and Broadmoor

Q156: In which army prison did the Krays serve their sentences for 'draft dodging'?
a: Colchester
b: Shepton Mallet
c: Aldershot
d: Tidworth

Q157: When were Ronnie and Reggie Kray born?
a: December 13 1933
b: October 24 1933
c: November 9 1932
d: September 2 1934

Q158: When did Ronnie Kray pass away?
    a: April 21 1998
    b: April 17 1995
    c: March 17 1995
    d: March 21 1998

Q159: When did Reggie Kray pass away?
    a: October 1 2000
    b: September 18, 2001
    c: August 16 1999
    d: November 1 1998

Q160: What was the name of the pub in which the murder of George Cornell took place?
    a: The Blind Beggar
    b: The Brooks
    c: Esmeralda's
    d: Carpenter's Arms

Q161: In what year were the Kray twins sentenced to a minimum recommendation of thirty years each?
    a: 1966
    b: 1967
    c: 1968
    d: 1969

Q162: Which Police Chief was responsible for the Kray twins' eventual downfall?
    a: Tommy Butler
    b: John Stalker
    c: Jack Sweeney
    d: Leonard Reed

Q163: Name the South London villain and leader of the team that carried out the Brinks Matt robbery at Heathrow.
a: Mickey McAvoy
b: Mickey McCarthy
c: Mickey 'Blue Eye' McCartney
d: Mickey McFinnigan

Q164: Both the Brinks Matt gang leader and another member of the team, Brian Robinson, received hefty sentences for their parts in the heist. How many years did each man get?
a: 15
b: 18
c: 25
d: 30

Q165: What is long-term prisoner Charlie Bronson's real name?
a: Michael Peterson
b: Mick Patterson
c: John Peterson
d: Mark Patterson

Q166: When was Charlie Bronson originally sent to prison, and what crime was it for?
a: 1972, robbery.
b: 1973, assault.
c: 1974, armed robbery.
d: 1975, robbery.

Q167: In which year did Charlie receive a life sentence at Luton Crown Court?
a: 1999
b: 2000
c: 2001
d: 2002

Q168: For what crime did Charlie receive a life sentence at Luton Crown Court?
a: Taking a civilian teacher hostage
b: Staging a rooftop protest
c: Conducting a prison siege
d: The attempted murder of a convicted sex offender

Q169: Charlie Bronson has been incarcerated for over three decades. How many prisons has he spent time in during this period?
a: 60+
b: 90+
c: 120+
d: 150+

Q170: Who received a life sentence with a thirty-year recommendation in 1966, for the murder of three policemen?
a: Harry Roberts
b: Harry Johnson
c: Harry Potter
d: Harry Jackson

RECENT PRISON FACTS

Q171: Today, the British Prison Service runs five main types of prison. Name them.
a: Local prisons, Young Offenders Institutions, Women's prisons, Lifers' prisons and High Security Prisons.
b: Open prisons, Young Offenders Institutions, Women's prisons, training prisons and High Security Prisons.
c: Local prisons, Young Persons Institutions, Women's prisons, training prisons and High Security Prisons.
d: Local prisons, Young Offenders Institutions, Women's prisons, training prisons and High Security Prisons.

Q172: When was the first British 'open prison' opened?
a: 1926
b: 1936
c: 1946
d: 1956

Q173: What was the name of the first 'open prison' in Britain?
a: New Hall Camp
b: New Hill Camp
c: New Camp Hill
d: New Hill Camp

Q174: The first British 'open prison' was opened as an 'annexe' to which established 'closed prison'?
a: Wakefield
b: Wandsworth
c: Leeds
d: Durham

Q175: Which of the following European countries has the highest prison population (per head)?
a: Germany
b: France
c: England and Wales
d: Denmark

Q176: How many privately-run prisons are there in England and Wales?
a: 11
b: 15
c: 19
d: 17

Q177: How many operational prisons are run by the public sector (ie. the Prison Service)?
a: 97
b: 113
c: 128
d: 136

Q178: One of the most serious criticisms of our prison system is that it has seen far too little improvement since the Victorian era. Most of our prisons were built in that era and remain largely unchanged. What percentage of today's prisons were built before 1980?
a: 95%
b: 88%
c: 97%
d: 85%

Q179: Which of these is not (nor has ever been) a real London prison?
a: Pentonville
b: Slade
c: The Houses of Parliament
d: The Wood Street Compter

Q180: True or false: HMP Latchmere House was once an MI5 interrogation centre.

Q181: In what year were the Parkhurst riots?
a: 1967
b: 1968
c: 1969
d: 1970

Q182: In 1971, a study of human responses to captivity and its behavioural effects on staff and inmates was carried out by students at which American university?
a: Yale
b: Harvard
c: Princetown
d: Stanford

Q183: True or false: The Criminal Justice Act of 1982 abolished the Borstal system.

Q184: What do the letters 'POA' stand for?
a: Principle Officer in Attendance
b: Prisoner On Adjudication
c: Prison Officers Association
d: Prison Officials Association

Q185: How many prisons are located on the Isle Of Wight, and what are they called?
a: 3: Parkhurst, Albany and Camp Hill.
b: 2: Parkhurst and Albany.
c: 2: Parkhurst and Camp Hill
d: 4: Parkhurst, Albany, South Sea ; and Camp Hill.

Q186: What is the name of the Portsmouth Prison for inmates serving life sentences?
a: Pompey Prison
b: Portland Bill
c: Kingston
d: South Port

Q187: What are the names of the six adult prisons in the London area?
a: Brixton, Pentonville, Wandsworth, Wormwood Scrubs, Belmarsh and Holloway.
b:Brixton, Pentonville, The Grange, Wormwood Scrubs, Belmarsh and Holloway.
c: Brixton, Cookham Wood, Wandsworth, Wormwood   Scrubs, Belmarsh and Holloway.
d: Brixton, Pentonville, Wandsworth, Wormwood Scrubs, Belmarsh and Long Lartin.

Q188: Which maximum security prison was the first to have an electronically-operated cell door installed?
a: Belmarsh
b: Brixton
c: Full Sutton
d: Albany

Q189: What is the name of Britain's most maximum security category A prison?
a: Belmarsh
b: Woodhill
c: Full Sutton
d: Frankland

Q190: Which prison saw the longest ever prison riot in the history of the Prison Service?
a: Parkhurst
b: Strangeways
c: Leeds
d: Wormwood Scrubs

Q191: What are the four different categories of Britain's prisons?
a: Category A, B, C and D.
b: High, medium, low and open.
c: AA, A, B and C - D.
d: There are now actually five categories, due to the terrorist threat. These are: Double A category, A category, B category, C category and D category.

Q192: What is currently the average cost of keeping an individual incarcerated for one year?
a: £37,500
b: £28,000
c: £29,000
d: £30,000

Q193: Which is London's largest prison (in terms of the number of inmates it can hold)?
a: Belmarsh
b: Brixton
c: Wormwood Scrubs
d: Wandsworth

Q194: Which is the largest prison in the country?
a: Frankland
b: Durham
c: Liverpool
d: Leicester

Q195: What is Parkhurst's official name?
   a: Central Prison
   b: Island Prison
   c: Barrack Prison
   d: Sea View Prison

Q196: What was known as 'Fraggle Rock' by staff and
   inmates, after the popular 80s puppet TV show?
   a: Brixton Prison Hospital
   b: Broadmoor
   c: Belmarsh Healthcare Unit
   d: GH&K Wings Wandsworth

Q197: How many prisoners successfully escaped from
   Parkhurst in 1995? (One of the escapees was an
   amateur pilot named Keith Rose who planned to
   escape the island by stealing a plane from a
   nearby air club.)
   a: 3
   b: 4
   c: 5
   d: 6

Q198: During what decade were the three prisons on the
   Isle of Wight downgraded from high security
   status?
   a: 1970s
   b: 1980s
   c: 1990s
   d: 2000s

Q199: When were the major riots in Dartmoor?
a: 1930
b: 1931
c: 1932
d: 1933

Q200: Who officially owns HMP Dartmoor?
a: The Duchy of Cornwall
b: The Queen
c: The Home Office
d: Group 4

Q201: When were the famous Strangeways riots?
a: 1989
b: 1990
c: 1991
d: 1992

Q202: What was the function of Parkhurst (on the Isle of Wight) before it became a prison?
a: A hospital
b: A barracks
c: A retirement home
d: A workhouse

Q203: The 'Birdman' was imprisoned in which famous prison?
a: Tamworth Castle
b: The Bastille
c: Alcatraz
d: Parkhurst

Q204: What is a 'kishka'?
    a: A prison cell
    b: A homemade weapon used by prisoners
    c: A weapon used by officers
    d: An inmate's secret stash of contraband

Q205: Which of the following is another word for jail?
    a: The Big House
    b: The Beak
    c: The Clink
    d: The Manor

Q206: Which of the following is an infamous American prison?
    a: Sing Sing
    b: Shout Shout
    c: Hum Hum
    d: Ding Ding

Q207: What is the official Home Office definition of a category A prisoner?
    a: Category A prisoners are those whose escape would be highly dangerous to the public or national security.
    b: Category A prisoners are those whose escape could be dangerous to the public or national security.
    c: Category A prisoners are those who *could* escape and would be highly dangerous to the public or national security.
    d: Category A prisoners are those whose escape would be highly dangerous to the public or *world* security.

Q208: What is the official Home Office definition of a category B prisoner?

a: Category B prisoners are those who don't require as much security, but for whom escape needs to be made very difficult.

b: Category B prisoners are those who don't really require any security, but for whom escape needs to be made very difficult.

c: Category B prisoners are those who don't require maximum security, but for whom escape needs to be made very difficult.

d: Category B prisoners are those who still require high security, and for whom escape needs to be made very difficult.

Q209: What is the official Home Office definition of a category C prisoner?

a: Category C prisoners are those who can be trusted in open conditions, but who are likely to try to escape.

b: Category C prisoners are those who can't be trusted in open conditions, but who are unlikely to try to escape.

c: Category C prisoners are those who can't be trusted in open conditions, and who are likely to try to escape.

d: Category C prisoners are those who can soon be trusted in open conditions, but who need more rehabilitation before they are unlikely to try to escape.

Q210: What is the official Home Office definition of a category D prisoner?
a: Category D prisoners are trusted enough to wander freely within the prison, but must not leave the prison grounds.
b: Category D prisoners are trusted enough to wander freely outside the prison, but must show up for several daily roll-calls.
c: Category D prisoners are trusted enough to wander freely both within the prison and outside, but must show up for a daily roll-call.
d: Category D prisoners are trusted enough to wander freely within the prison, but must show up for several daily roll-calls.

Q211: Who is the Chief Inspector of Prisons?
a: A publicly-elected figure who reports on prison conditions.
b: Someone independent of the Prison Service who reports on prison conditions.
c: A Prison Service employee
d: An MP

Q212: What do the letters 'NEPO' stand for?
a: Newly executed prisoner/offender
b: Non-executive punishment order
c: New entrant Prison Officer
d: New executive prison orders

Q213: What do the letters 'HCO' stand for?
a: Health Care Officer
b: Hospital Care Officer
c: Hospital Care Orderly
d: Health Care Operative

Q214: How many 'Governor grades' are there (not including acting governors)?
a: 1
b: 3
c: 5
d: 6

Q215: What is the correct order of rank for today's Prison Service Uniformed Landing Officers?
a: Prison Officer, Senior Officer, Principle Officer
b: Prison Officer, Senior Officer, Chief Officer
c: Auxiliary Officer, Senior Officer, Principle Officer
d: Prison Officer, Senior Officer, Principle Officer, Chief Officer

Q216: True or False: The rank of Chief Officer was removed from the Prison Service in an attempt to demilitarise the service?

Q217: Prison staff were taught 'drill' at their prison service colleges, and put on a military-style 'passing out parade' for their friends and relatives on the last day of training. In what year was this stopped in an attempt to demillitarise the service?
a: 1988
b: 1990
c: 1992
d: 1996

Q218: Which high security prison, in 1991, embarrassingly lost a prisoner, when he walked out of the visits hall, unchallenged by any prison staff?
a: Belmarsh
b: Durham
c: Long Lartin
d: Wakefield

Q219: What are the main duties of the Wing Cleaning Officer?
a: Cleaning the wing
b: Making sure all the prisoners get showers and wash their clothes
c: Supervising outside work parties
d: Organising and supervising the wing's general daily administration

Q220: What is an 'accumulated visit'?
a: When a prisoner too far from home for his family to visit saves up his visits entitlement
b: When a prisoner saves his visits and has them all together on the last weekend of each month
c: When a prisoner saves his weekly visits and has one long visit every Saturday or Sunday
d: When a prisoner gives his visits entitlement to another prisoner

Q221: True or false: A prisoner serving time in a jail far away from his home and family can request a temporary transfer to a more local jail in order to take his accumulated visits - if he pays for the transport himself.

Q222: The process described in Q221 for temporarily transferring prisoners to local jails is known by what name?
a: The accumulator
b: The visits merry-go-round
c: A lie down
d: A turn around

Q223: What is a 'closeting chain'?
a: A chain for securing the wing ablutions
b: The name for the line of men walking along the landing to empty their slop buckets
c: A chain used to secure the doors in a prisoner transport van
d: A chain with three individual handcuffs attached for use during prison escorts

Q224: What is a 'closeting chain' officially used for?
a: Allowing prisoners more space when being escorted from A to B
b: Shackling two prisoners together
c: Securing a particularly high escape-risk prisoner's legs together so he can barely walk
d: Allowing a prisoner to go to the toilet during an escort whilst remaining securely attached to the officer outside the door

Q225: What is the name of the national newspaper for prisons?
a: Inside Times
b: Insider Times
c: Prison Weekly
d: Prison News

Q226: When was the national newspaper for prisons first published?
a: 1988
b: 1990
c: 1994
d: 1997

Q227: In which year did the national newspaper for prisons celebrate its 100th edition?
a: 1998
b: 2000
c: 2004
d: 2007

CELEBRITY PRISONERS

Q228: Johnny Cash famously recorded an album whilst in prison. What was his nickname?
a: The Man in Pink
b: The Man in Black
c: The Man in Agony
d: The Man in a Van

Q229: Which famous jockey was sentenced to three years in prison for tax evasion?
a: Frankie Dettorri
b: Willie Carson
c: Lester Piggott
d: Paddy McCarthy

Q230: What British, ex-boxing champion stood trial for shooting boxing promoter, Frank Warren?
a: Charlie Magri
b: Terry Marsh
c: Nigel Benn
d: Sammy McCarthy

Q231: Which well-known British actor was involved in running protection rackets and acquitted of the murder of John Darke in 1979?
a: John Bindon
b: Donald Sinden
c: Bob Hoskins
d: Jack Lyddon

Q232: Name the famous singer who served a sentence in Wormwood Scrubs in the nineties for possession of an offensive weapon.
a: George Michael
b: Mark 'the Mac' Morrison
c: Pete Doherty
d: Liam Gallagher

Q233: What British ex-champion boxer received an eighteen-year prison sentence for armed robbery?
a: Terry Spinks
b: Sammy McCarthy
c: Jimmy Batten
d: Joe Crickmar

Q234: Which Conservative MP and Lord received a seven year custodial sentence for perjury?
a: John Major
b: Norman Tebbitt
c: Jeffrey Archer
d: Allen Clarke

Q235: Name the Conservative minister who, in 1999, was jailed for eighteen months.
a: Jonathan Aitken
b: Robert Atkins
c: Max Aitken
d: William Aitken

Q236: Which of the following Lords has also served a custodial prison sentence?
a: Lord Brocket
b: Lord Such
c: Lord Brody
d: Lord Bath

Q237: Who was the professional racing driver involved in 'the Great Train Robbery'?
a: Jackie Stewart
b: Roy James
c: James Hunt
d: James Irvine

Q238: Which world-famous ex-Manchester-United footballer spent time as an inmate in Ford open prison?
a: Roy Keane
b: Eric Cantona
c: George Best
d: Dennis Law

Q239: What was Lord Brocket convicted of in 1996?
a: Conspiracy to commit car insurance fraud
b: Perjury
c: Perverting the course of justice
d: Dangerous driving whilst banned

Q240: What occured in Bedford Prison shortly after Lord Brocket's conviction that resulted in his being transferred to Ford Prison?
a: He was caught in possession of an illegal substance
b: He assaulted a member of staff
c: He had his sentence reduced
d: He was stabbed by a fellow inmate

Q241: Lord Brocket is lucky enough to have been given a part in Dave Courtney's film about the club scene. The film is called 'Clubbing to Death' and is due for release in 2008. In the film, what character does Brocket play?
a: A clubber
b: A policeman
c: Himself
d: A gangster

PRISON-RELATED FILM AND TELEVISION

Q242: In TV series, 'The Prisoner', which character was played by the actor Patrick McGoohan?
a: Number Two
b: Number Four
c: Number Six
d: Number Nine

Q243: Who played the main character in the original movie, 'Mean Machine', that featured an American football player jailed in a tough American state penitentiary?
a: Burt Lancaster
b: Burt Reynolds
c: Charlton Heston
d: Richard Burton

Q244: The original version of the graphically-violent Ray Winstone film, 'Scum', was intended for TV but banned by the censors. In what year was the film version released in cinemas?
a: 1976
b: 1977
c: 1978
d: 1979

Q245: Who played 'Danny Meehan', the jailed professional footballer, in the 90s British remake of hit film, 'Mean Machine'?
a: Jason Statham
b: Vinnie Jones
c: Ronnie Barker
d: Martin Kemp

Q246: Who played the Kray twins in the film, 'The Krays'?
a: Phil and Gary Neville
b: Matt and Luke Goss
c: Vinnie Jones and Jason Statham
d: Martin and Gary Kemp

Q247: Which 80s, chart-busting brothers played the Richardson brothers in 'Charlie'?
a: The Goss brothers
b: The Righteous Brothers
c: The Kemp brothers
d: The Proclaimers

Q248: Who played 'Bacon' in the gangster film, 'Lock, Stock and Two Smoking Barrels', and 'Turkish' in 'Snatch'?
a: Vinnie Jones
b: Jason Statham
c: Brad Pitt
d: Jason Flemyng

Q249: Name the two main Prison Officers in the cult 70s prison series, ' Porridge'.

Q250: Name 'Porridge's main character and the actor who plays him.

Q251: Name the actor who was one half of a famous 80s TV duo and played an 'old lag' in 'Porridge'.
a: Ronnie Corbett
b: Eddie Large
c: David Jason
d: Eric Morecambe

Q252: Which famous underworld figure was the inspiritation for Vinnie Jones' character, 'Bullet Tooth Tony', in 'Lock, Stock and Two Smoking Barrels'?
a: Frank Fraser
b: Lennie MacLean
c: Dave Courtney
d: Roy 'Pretty Boy' Shaw

Q253: Which female celebrity was married to underworld legend, Ronnie Knight?
a: Barbara Cartland
b: Barbara Windsor
c: Barbara Streisand
d: Barbara Stanwyck

Q254: Which long-running, Australian prison drama was set in the fictitious Wentworth Prison?
a: Prisoner Cell Block H
b: The Colony
c: Wentworth CC
d: The Outback

Q255: What is the name of Lynda La Plant's popular TV drama about a women's prison?
a: Bad Uns
b: Bad Girls
c: Women behind Bars
d: Black Widows

Q256: In what prison was cult TV show, 'Porridge', set?
a: Glade
b: Blade
c: Slade
d: Wade

Q257: Which well-known TV personality spent time in Strangeways on a fraud charge before becoming famous?
a: Leslie Grantham
b: Jimmy Nail
c: Ricky Tomlinson
d: David Dickinson

Q258: Which EastEnders actor spent time in prison for manslaughter before he became a star?
a: Steve McFadden
b: Ross Kemp
c: Leslie Grantham
d: Bill Murray

Q259: Name the 1960 'Ealing Comedy' that stars Peter Sellers, Lionel Jeffries and Bernard Cribbins as a group of prisoners who scheme to break out of jail, commit a robbery and then break back in.
a: 'Two Way Mirror'
b: 'Two Way Ticket'
c: 'Two Way Stretch'
d: 'Two Way Road'

Q260: On the life of which gangland icon was the 1979 British film, 'The Long Good Friday', based?
a: Freddie Foreman
b: Frank Fraser
c: Charlie Richardson
d: Ronnie Kray

Q261: Which well-known actor played 'Freddie Foreman' in 'The Long Good Friday'?
a: Michael Cane
b: Oliver Reed
c: Bob Hoskins
d: Ray Winstone

Q262: Name the actor set to play Charlie Bronson in the 2008 film about his life.
a: Tom Cruise
b: Tom Arnold
c: Tom Hardy
d: Tom Hanks

Q263: Name the hit 70s film in which Michael Caine plays a London gangster who ventures up to the North East to avenge his brother's death at the hands of a gangster.
a: Get Lost
b: Get Going
c: Get Out
d: Get Carter

Q264: Michael Caine plays an ex-convict, alongside Benny Hill, in a 60s film classic that involves three Minis. What was the film called?
a: The Spaghetti Job
b: The Italian Job
c: The Pizza Delivery Job
d: The Pasta Job

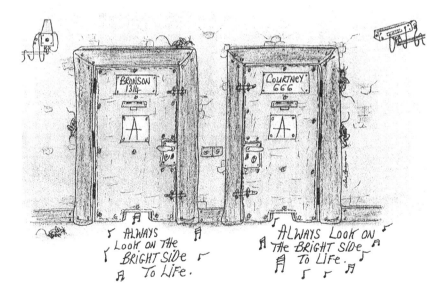

PRISON PUNISHMENTS

Q265: What was a 'pillory'?
a: An early form of segregation where inmates were placed in cells padded with pillows
b: A metal frame used to encase prisoners and then suspended from a post as a form of public humiliation
c: A form of medieval stocks in which a petty criminal is locked by the head and hands for public humiliation
d: An early type of public flogging post that was so named because, when cut down, prisoners would often be laid on beds of feather by friends or family to ease their abrasions

Q266: Samuel Cubitt was responsible for devising which prison punishment?
a: The Treadwheel
b: The Crank
c: The 'separate system'
d: Birching

Q267: Which English prison was the first to 'work' the prisoners on the Treadwheel?
a: Brixton
b: Ludgate
c: Wormwood Scrubs
d: Milbank

Q268: What was the rate of climb that prisoners were
expected to achieve on the Treadwheel?
a: 20-30 steps per minute
b: 25-35 steps per minute
c: 36-38 steps per minute
d: 48-50 steps per minute

Q269: In which prison was the last Treadwheel (prior to its
being was dismantled in 1907)?
a: York Castle Prison
b: Wandsworth
c: Tower of London
d: Durham Prison

Q270: Which year saw the abolition of the 'Bread and
Water' punishment?
a: 1959
b: 1963
c: 1968
d: 1971

Q271: Sewing mailbags (an old punishment) was a
laborious and extremely tedious task that had to be
carried out with exact precision. What was the
regulation number of stitches per inch?
a: 4 stitches to every inch
b: 6 stitches to every inch
c: 5 stitches to every inch
d: 3 stitches to every inch

Q272: What colour are the overalls that prisoners on the 'escape list' and category A prisoners on escort have to wear?
a: Yellow and green striped
b: Blue and white striped
c: Grey and black with arrows on it
d: There aren't any overalls. Prisoners just wear their normal prison uniforms.

Q273: In prison rules, what does 'GOAD' stand for?
a: Governor on adjudication duty
b: Good order and discipline
c: Gym orderly and detainee
d: Get out after dinner

Q274: What year saw the abolition of the 'separate system'?
a: 1908
b: 1919
c: 1922
d: 1926

Q275: What is the maximum amount of time that a prisoner should be on 'cellular confinement' before review by a Governor?
a: Five days
b: Six days
c: Fourteen days
d: Four days

Q276: What is the official name of the hearing often referred to by prisoners as 'a kangaroo court', in which an inmate charged with breaking prison rules is seen by a Governor to be punished?
a: Prison Orders
b: An Adjudication Hearing
c: Governors Orders
d: Inmate Punishment Hearing

Q277: What is Prison Rule 45?
a: Rule 45 concerns the segregation of vulnerable prisoners.
b: Rule 45 concerns the segregation of young prisoners.
c: Rule 45 concerns the segregation of prisoners as punishment for escaping.
d: Rule 45 concerns the segregation of terrorist prisoners.

Q278: In what year was 'birching' abolished as a punishment in British prisons?
a: 1960
b: 1961
c: 1962
d: 1963

Q279: What is the maximum amount of time a prisoner can be segregated from the normal wing for reasons of ensuring good order and discipline before it has to be reviewed?
a: 7 days
b: 14 days
c: 21 days
d: 28 days

Q280: In 1951, an order was given that all UK male prisons were to use only 'birches' and cat o' nine tails from a national stock. In which of the following prisons was the stock kept?
a: Wandsworth
b: Brixton
c: Pentonville
d: Wormwood Scrubs

Q281: Which infamous prisoner was the last ever British inmate to be flogged with the cat o' nine tails?
a: Frank Fraser
b: Eric Mason
c: Charlie Bronson
d: Roy Shaw

Q282: A paralysing drug is known to be frequently administered to 'patients' of the special hospitals (and some prison hospitals) who are considered 'difficult' to handle - although this is denied by the authorities. What name do inmates give to this drug?
a: The Liquid Cosh
b: The Liquid Bosh
c: The Liquid Slosh
d: The Liquid Squash

Q283: What is the name of the form that must be given to prisoners to explain the process of adjudication?
a: F1792
b: F1642
c: F111
d: F1145

Q284: An adult prisoner found guilty on adjudication can be cautioned and/or given one or more of five other punishments. What are they?
a: Loss of privileges, stoppage of earnings, cellular confinement, added days and exclusion from work
b: Loss of association, stoppage of earnings, cellular confinement, added days and exclusion from work
c: Loss of privileges, stoppage of earnings, solitary confinement, added days and exclusion from work
d: Loss of privileges, stoppage of earnings, cellular confinement, added days and additional work

Q285: If an adult is punished with a loss of earnings, loss of privileges or added days, what is the maximum number of days that this can extend for?
a: 21
b: 28
c: 42
d: 56

Q286: What is the maximum number of days a prisoner can be excluded from work for as a punishment for breaking prison rules?
a: 7
b: 14
c: 21
d: 28

Q287: If a prisoner under the age of 21 is punished with a loss of earnings, loss of privileges or added days, what is the maximum number of days this can extend for?
a: 21
b: 28
c: 42
d: 56

Q288: How many offences against prison discipline are listed in the prison rule book?
a: 19
b: 21
c: 25
d: 28

Q289: Which rule sets out all the offences against prison discipline?
a: Rule 51
b: Rule 28
c: Rule 19
d: Rule 56

Q290: True or false: Rules for adults and young offenders that cover offences against prison discipline include 'catch all' offences that cover a wide variety of rule-breaking.

PRISON SLANG

Q291: What is prison slang for "being locked up"?

Q292: In a prison environment, who or what is 'The Baron'?

Q293: What is prison slang for 'prison sentence'?

Q294: 'Beef' has two meanings in prison. What are they?

Q295: Define 'a cell soldier'.

Q296: Who or what is a 'kanga'?

Q297: What would a prisoner be referring to if he mentioned his 'Peter'?

Q298: If a prisoner did not get a result that he was hoping for (for example: on an appeal, or an application for a move or re-categorisation), how might he state this?
a: "I got turned down"
b: "They said no again"
c: "I got a knock-back"
d: "I was stitched up"

Q299: If a prisoner said he was up for 'Jam Role', what would he be waiting for?

Q300: If an Officer or prisoner said, "He's down the hole", where would 'he' be?

Q301: What is referred to as a 'Durham nip'?

Q302: If you were asked for a 'tailor-made', what would you be expected to hand over?

Q303: What sort of person is one described as a 'nonce'?

Q304: What is a 'grass'?

Q305: What is the commonly used name for a prison cell van?
a: Sweat Box
b: Armoured Car
c: Strong Box
d: Black Mariah

Q306: What would be happening if someone were said to be 'clucking'?
a: Someone is high on drugs
b: Someone is coming off drugs
c: Someone is informing the staff about other prisoners behaviour on the wing
d: Someone is going slightly mad due to being locked up

Q307: What is 'the Judas Hole'?
a: A segregation cell for grasses
b: The prison chapel
c: The spy hole on a cell door
d: The waste disposal unit where staff flush
confiscated drugs away

Q308: Who are referred to by prisoners as 'the burglars'?
a: Prisoners who steal from fellow inmates' cells
b: Dedicated staff cell-searching teams
c: Prisoners who steal extra rations or other items
from staff areas
d: Staff who have been conditioned to bring in
contraband for prisoners

Q309: Who or what is 'the Mufti'?
a: An underground prisoner vigilante group
b: The store man responsible for handing out cold
weather gear for outside work parties
c: The specially-trained riot squads
d: The wing 'porn baron'

Q310: What does 'hooch' refer to?
a: Prison dogs
b: Solitary cells
c: A potent alcoholic brew made in secret by
prisoners
d: Prisoners' secret stash of contraband

Q311: What is a 'shit parcel'?
a: A parcel sent in by a relative that contains useless items
b: The trolley containing the wing's laundry wrapped in bundles with brown prison sheets
c: An Officer getting a slop bucket thrown over him by a prisoner
d: Human waste, wrapped in paper and thrown out of a cell window during the night

Q312: What is a 'merry-go-round'?
a: When a prisoner is moved from one prison to another, in quick succession and without prior knowledge, for reasons of ensuring good order and discipline
b: A game prisoners play on the pool table during association
c: The phrase used to describe the practice of prisoners taking daily exercise that consists solely of walking around the yard for an hour in the same direction
d: When staff distribute (or 'go round') the wing with the 'merry trolley' that contains prescribed drugs for certain prisoners

SEX OFFENDERS IN PRISON

Q313: Name the establishment where 'Moors murderer',
Ian Brady, is currently held.
a: Broadmoor Special Hospital
b: Ashworth Special Hospital
c: Rampton Special Hospital
d: Wakefield Special Hospital

Q314: Who is the longest-serving, category A prisoner
incarcerated for sex offences in England?
a: Peter Sutcliffe
b: Ian Huntley
c: John Straffen
d: Ian Brady

Q315: How many women was Peter Sutcliffe convicted of
killing?
a: 10
b: 11
c: 12
d: 13

Q316: In what case did 'Wearside Jack' give police false
information that seriously hindered their
investigation?
a: The Jack the Ripper case
b: The Yorkshire Ripper case
c: The Moors Murders case
d: The Soham Murders case

Q317: In which institution is Rose West currently held?
   a: Bronzefield
   b: Parc
   c: Cookham Wood
   d: Askham Grange

Q318: How many years did Myra Hyndley spend in prison?
   a: 30
   b: 35
   c: 39
   d: 37

Q319: Myra Hyndley died on the June 15 2002, aged 60. Where was she at the time of her death?
   a: West Suffolk Hospital
   b: Chatham Maritime Hospital
   c: Cookham Wood Prison Hospital
   d: Broadmoor Special Hospital

Q320: True or false: At the time of her death, Myra Hyndley was Britain's longest-serving female prisoner.

Q321: Who was Dr Shipman's first victim?
   a: His mother
   b: His first wife
   c: An elderly patient (while he was a junior doctor)
   d: No one knows.

Q322: True or false: Dr Shipman admitted his crimes.

Q323: What is the title of the book Nilsen wrote about his life in prison?
a: Evil Love
b: Killing For Company
c: The Drowning Man
d: A Strangled Life

Q324: What is the name of Nilsen's defence lawyer?
a: Ivan Lawrence QC
b: Brian Masters QC
c: Allen Green QC
d: John Croom-Johnson QC

Q325: How were Nilsen's murders discovered?
a: By his mother
b: By his partner
c: One of his victims escaped and raised the alarm
d: By a plumber called in to clear a blocked drain

Q326: Which 70s pop star was jailed in 1999 for possession of child pornography?

Q327: Upon his release, Glitter fled to Vietnam, but was jailed again on March 3 2006. What was the charge and how long was the prison sentence he received?
a: Committing obscene acts with men, for which he received a three-year prison sentence
b: Committing obscene acts with minors, for which he received a three-year prison sentence
c: Committing obscene acts with minors, for which he received a five-year prison sentence
d: Committing obscene acts with animals, for which he received a two-year prison sentence

Q328: Sarah Payne went missing on July 1 2000, while on her way to visit her grandparents in Kingston Gorse in Sussex. Who was convicted of her highly publicised murder?
a: Roy Whiting
b: Geoff Whiting
c: Rob Whiting
d: Trevor Whiting

Q329: Sarah Payne's murderer was attacked in prison by Rickie Tregaskis (himself a convicted murderer). Where did this attack take place?
a: Whitemoor
b: Wandsworth
c: Wakefield
d: Long Lartin

HIGH-RISK LIFE-SENTENCED PRISONERS

Q330: What is an 'automatic lifer'?
a: A person aged 18 or over, sentenced to life for a second serious sexual or violent offence committed on or after October 1 1997
b: A person aged 18 or over, sentenced to life for a first serious sexual or violent offence committed on or after October 1 1997
c: A person aged 18 or under, sentenced to life for a first serious sexual or violent offence committed on or after October 1 1999
d: A person aged 18 or over, sentenced to life for a second serious sexual or violent offence committed on or after October 31 1997

Q331: What is a 'discretionary life sentence'?
a: A life sentence given for any serious offence (including murder), which is not a 'mandatory' sentence
b: A life sentence given for a serious offence committed in prison (other than murder), which is not a 'mandatory' sentence
c: A life sentence given for a serious offence (other than murder), which is not a 'mandatory' sentence
d: A life sentence given for a serious offence (other than murder) to a person already serving a sentence of five years or more, which is not a 'mandatory' sentence.

Q332: What do the letters 'DLP' stand for?
a: Discretionary Lifer Panel
b: Disco for Lifer Prisoners
c: Detained Life Prisoner
d: Deranged Life Prisoner

Q333: What is a 'mandatory life sentence'?
a: The sentence a court must give any man convicted of murder
b: The sentence a court must give anyone convicted of murder or any other serious offence
c: The sentence a court must give anyone convicted of murder, unless there are special mitigating circumstances
d: The sentence a court must give anyone convicted of murder

Q334: What is the 'Lifer Unit'?
a: The part of the prison that deals with the management and reviews of all lifer cases
b: The part of the Prison Service Headquarters (based at Abel house, London) that deals with the management and reviews of all lifer cases
c: The part of the Crown Prosecution Service (based in London) that deals with the arrangement of all court cases that could potentially result in a life sentence
d: The part of the prison where all lifers are accommodated

Q335: What is a 'tariff'?

a: The part of a prisoner's life sentence that must be served in prison as both a punishment for them and a deterrent to others. (It is extremely rare that a prisoner is ever released before their tariff date.)

b: The part of a prisoner's life sentence that must be served in prison as both a punishment for them and a deterrent to others, where prisoners are allowed town visits and given a 'tariff' (or token) to present to police if they are stopped in the street.

c: The part of a prisoner's life sentence that must be served in prison as both a punishment for them and a deterrent to others - but that is served in a hostel-type building, just inside the prison, where they are treated in semi-open conditions.

d: The part of a prisoner's life sentence that must be served in prison as both a punishment for them and a deterrent to others, but where they are issued with a 'tariff' that allows them to 'clock ! in and out' of the prison during the times specified on their individual tariff.

Q336: According to the prison handbook, there are currently five category A Dispersal Prisons that house high-risk, long-term prisoners in England and Wales. Which prisons are they?

a: Belmarsh, Frankland, Parkhurst, Whitemoor and Wakefield

b: Long Lartin, Full Sutton, Durham, Wakefield and Belmarsh

c: Frankland, Full Sutton, Long Lartin, Wakefield and Whitemoor

d: Full Sutton, Long Lartin, Whitemoor, Frankland and Belmarsh

Q337: What are the three prisons in England and Wales that are classed as 'super max' prisons?
a: Belmarsh, Frankland and Wakefield
b: Wakefield, Belmarsh and Long Lartin
c: Belmarsh, Whitemoor and Wakefield
d: Belmarsh, Whitemoor and Parkhurst

Q338: Which establishment is currently the largest maximum security prison in England and Wales?
a: Wakefield
b: Whitemoor
c: Long Lartin
d: Frankland

Q339: What do the letters 'LSP' stand for?
a: Long Serving Prisoner
b: Life Sentence Plan
c: Life Sentence Prisoner
d: Last Sentenced Prisoner

Q340: What is an 'escorted absence'?
a: This is where category C lifers, subject to certain conditions, undertake familiarisation visits to a local town under the supervision of a Prison Officer.
b: This is where category C lifers subject to certain conditions, undertake familiarisation visits to a local town under the supervision of a Prison Officer or person from his approved visitors list.
c: This is where category B lifers, subject to certain conditions, undertake familiarisation visits to a local town under the supervision of a Prison Officer.
d: This is where category D lifers, subject to certain conditions, undertake familiarisation visits to a local town under the supervision of a Prison Officer.

Q341: What is a 'First Stage Prison'?
a: A prison that specialises in accommodating lifers for the first four to six years of their sentences
b: A prison that specialises in assessing newly convicted lifers to see which lifer prison would best suit their needs
c: A prison that specialises in assessing newly convicted lifers and preparing their Life Sentence Plans
d: A prison that specialises in assessing newly convicted lifers between the ages of 18 and 21, and preparing their Life Sentence Plans

Q342: What is a 'Second Stage Prison'?
a: A prison that specialises in accommodating lifers during the main parts of their sentences (usually category B or C)
b: A prison that specialises in accommodating lifers during the main parts of their sentences (usually category A or B)
c: A prison that specialises in accommodating lifers during the main part of their sentences (usually category C or D)
d: A prison that specialises in accommodating lifers who are serving a second consecutive life sentence (usually category A)

Q343: In 1994, six members of the IRA escaped from a top security British prison, using firearms. Which prison was it?
a: Woodhill
b: Belmarsh
c: Whitemoor
d: Long Lartin

BASIC PRISON RULES AND REGULATIONS

Q344: How many people are allowed to visit a convicted
prisoner or prisoner on remand at any given time?
a: 2
b: 3
c: 4
d: 5

Q345: How often can an unconvicted prisoner on remand
have visits?
a: Every working day (ie. Monday to Friday) or at
least three of these days, during the periods in
which visiting hours normally take place
b: Once a week
c: Twice a week
d: Once a fortnight

Q346: For which three days a year are there no prison
visits?
a: Christmas Eve, Christmas Day and Boxing Day
b: Christmas Day, Boxing Day and New Years Eve
c: Christmas Day, Boxing Day and Good Friday
d: Christmas Day, Boxing Day and Easter Sunday

Q347: What is the minimum number of visits that a convicted prisoner is entitled to every four weeks?
a: 1
b: 2
c: 3
d: 4

Q348: Any prisoner found bringing illegal drugs into the prison (via his visits) can expect to have how many days added to his sentence?
a: Up to 14
b: Up to 28
c: Up to 36
d: Up to 42

Q349: In addition to the days added to his sentence, a prisoner found bringing illegal drugs into the prison (via visits) can expect to become subject to closed visits. How long is this punishment likely to extend?
a: Three months
b: Four months
c: Five months
d: Six months

Q350: How many free letters does an unconvicted prisoner receive (to send out) each week?
a: 1
b: 2
c: 3
d: 4

Q351: How many free letters does a convicted prisoner receive (to send out) each week?
a: 1
b: 2
c: 3
d: 1 per day

Q352: What is Prison Rule 39 concerned with?
a: The placing of prisoners on closed visits, following allegations of smuggling in contraband via visits
b: The monitoring and taping of an inmate's phone calls, due to intelligence received on that inmate
c: The banning of a visitor from an establishment, following an incident involving them or the prisoner they were visiting
d: The allowing of legal documents to be posted to inmates without being opened and/or read

Q353: True or false: Inmates are permitted to write letters in any language.

Q354: What do the letters 'CARAT' stand for?
a: Category A Rehabilitation and Treatment
b: Category A Relocation and Transportation
c: Counselling, Advice, Referral, Assessment and Thorough Care
d: Counselling, Advice on Rehabilitation Assessments and Tracking

Q355: According to prisoner and staff handbooks, how many offences are there that a prisoner can be charged with?
a: 18
b: 25
c: 28
d: 32

Q356: Which form gives a prisoner the details of an offense against prison discipline that they are to be charged with?
a: F1127
b: F111
c: F2045
d: F2711

Q357: What do the letters 'ARD' stand for?
a: Active Rehabilitation of a Detainee
b: Actual Rehabilitation of a Detainee
c: Actual Release Date
d: Active Release Date

Q358: With sentences of twelve months or less, how much of the sentence will a prisoner who has shown 'good behaviour' in prison actually serve?
a: A third
b: Half
c: Two thirds
d: Three quarters

Q359: What do the letters 'SED' stand for?
a: Sentence Expiry Date
b: Solitary Expiry Date
c: Sentence Extended Days
d: Solitary Extended Days

Q360: When should a newly convicted prisoner be informed of his ADR and SED?
a: Within a week of sentencing
b: As soon as the paperwork arrives from the court
c: One working day after sentencing
d: On arrival in prison, immediately after sentencing

Q361: What do the letters 'HDC' stand for?
a: Home Office Detention Certificate
b: Home Detention Certificate
c: Home Office Detention Curfew
d: Home Detention Curfew

Q362: What do the letters 'CRD' stand for?
a: Conditional Release Date
b: Confidential Reform Details
c: Conditional Rehabilitation Details
d: Conditional Re-Categorisation Details

Q363: If a sentence is between twelve months and four years, at what point do any conditions set for early release (such as supervision orders) expire?
a: Halfway point
b: One-third point
c: Three-quarter point
d: Two-thirds point

Q364: What do the letters 'PED' stand for?
a: Parole Eligibility Date
b: Parole Expiry Date
c: Punishment Expiry Date
d: Prisoners Eligibility Date

Q365: All prisoners - regardless of the length of their sentence - could be subject to 'ADA's. What does this acronym stand for?
a: Added Days Awarded
b: Additional Days Awarded
c: Awarded Days Added
d: Additional Detention Awarded

Q366: There are three regimes for prisoners, with allocation dependent upon behaviour, job status, etc. What are they?
a: Basic, standard and enhanced
b: Low, medium and high
c: Poor, good and exceptional
d: 2 star, 3 star and 4 star

Q367: Money brought in by prisoners or sent to them by outside parties is known by what name?
a: Private stash
b: Personal monies
c: Private cash
d: Prisoners monies

Q368: How much money is a convicted prisoner on the lowest regime permitted to spend in the canteen in a week?
a: £250
b: £500
c: £1000
d: £3000

Q369: How much money is a convicted prisoner on the middle regime permitted to spend in the canteen in a week?
a: £1250
b: £1500
c: £1000
d: £3000

Q370: How much money is a convicted prisoner on the highest regime permitted to spend in the canteen in a week?
a: £1250
b: £1500
c: £1000
d: £3000

Q371: Unconvicted prisoners are permitted to spend one of two amounts of money, depending on whether they are on the lowest regime or the middle or top regimes. What are these amounts?
a: £10 for prisoners on lowest regime, £20 for those on the middle and top regimes
b: £15 for prisoners on lowest regime, £40 for those on the middle and top regimes
c: £25 for prisoners on lowest regime, £50 for prisoners on the middle and top regimes
d: £15 for prisoners on lowest regime and £30 for those on the middle and top regimes

Q372: What are the three reasons a prisoner may be granted leave to appeal In the Court of Appeal?
a: The conviction is unsafe or unsatisfactory, there was a wrong decision on a question of law or a material irregularity in the course of the trial
b: The prisoner is unsafe or their behaviour unsatisfactory, there was a wrong decision on a question of law or a material irregularity in the course of the trial
c: The conviction is unsafe or unsatisfactory, there was a wrong decision on a question of how long the sentence should be or there was a material irregularity in the course of the trial
d: The conviction is unsafe or unsatisfactory, there was a wrong decision on a question of law or the accused was denied the chance of council in the course of the trial

Q373: At what intervals must staff physically check on prisoners who are on an 'at-risk watch' due to a high risk of self-harm or suicide?
a: Every 10 minutes
b: Every 15 minutes
c: Every 20 minutes
d: Every 30 minutes

WALES, SCOTLAND
AND IRELAND

Q374: One of Britain's last executioners was a Scotsman.
What was his name?
a: Robert Leslie Stewart
b: Stewart Leslie Robert
c: Leslie Robert Stewart
d: Robert Stewart Leslie

Q375: The executioner in Q374 carried out the last
execution in Wales. In which prison did that
execution take place?
a: Cardiff Prison
b: Bridgend Prison
c: Swansea Prison
d: Usk Prison

Q376: Wales' only convicted serial killer was sentenced to
life imprisonment In 1996. What was his name?
a: Patrick Moore
b: Paul Moore
c: Peter Moore
d: John Moore

Q377: The last execution carried out in Ireland was in 1961. In which prison did that execution take place?
a: Crumlin Road Prison
b: Maghaberry Prison
c: Armagh Prison
d: Magilligan Prison

Q378: The last execution carried out in Scotland was in 1963. In which prison did that execution take place?
a: Kilmarnock Prison
b: Aberdeen Prison
c: Edinburgh Prison
d: Barlinnie Prison

Q379: How many prisons are controlled by the Scottish Prison Service?
a: 10
b: 12
c: 15
d: 18

Q380: Scotland's most notorious prison is HMP Barlinnie. Where is it located?
a: Edinburgh
b: Glasgow
c: Aberdeen
d: Stirling

Q381: Scotland's most infamous serial killer, Peter Manuel, was charged and convicted in 1958. How many murders was he convicted of?
a: 7
b: 10
c: 12
d: 15

Q382: Peter Manuel was hanged at which Scottish prison in 1958?
a: Aberdeen
b: Barlinnie
c: Edinburgh
d: Kilmarnock

Q383: Who was the famous Irish Revolutionary was hanged for treason for his part in planning the 1916 Easter Rising?
a: Roger Casement
b: Eamon de Valera
c: Patrick Pearse
d: James Connolly

Q384: What crime were the 'Maguire Seven' wrongly convicted of in 1976?
a: Running a 'safe house' in Willesden, North London
b: Running a bomb-making factory
c: Organising the Birmingham bombing campaign
d: Providing training for terrorist operatives working in the UK

Q385: All but one of the 'Maguire Seven' served their entire sentences as imposed by the court. Which of the seven was the exception?
a: Anne Maguire
b: Patrick Maguire
c: Patrick 'Giuseppe' Conlon
d: Vincent Maguire

Q386: The story of the terrible miscarriages of justice and false imprisonment of the 'Guildford Four' and 'Maguire Seven' was told in which powerful film?
a: The Crying Game
b: Harry's Game
c: In The Name of the Father
d: The Innocence of Four

Q387: Which British Prime Minister issued a public apology to the 'Guildford Four' and 'Maguire Seven' for the injustice they suffered?
a: Margaret Thatcher
b: John Major
c: Tony Blair
d: Gordon Brown

Q388: Who was the female wrongly convicted of carrying out three major IRA bomb attacks in 1974?
a: Judith Ward
b: Julie Dougan
c: Mairead Farrell
d: Pauline Kane

Q389: The first hunger strike began as a blanket protest, and was started by Kieran Nugent in which year?
a: 1974
b: 1975
c: 1976
d: 1980

Q390: What were the five demands made by the prisoners involved in the first hunger strike?
a: The right not to wear a prison uniform; the right to do prison work; the right to free association with other prisoners and to organise educational and recreational pursuits; the right to one visit, one letter and one parcel per week; and full restoration of remission lost through the protest
b: The right not to wear a prison uniform; the right not to do prison work; the right to free association with other prisoners and to organise educational and recreational pursuits; the right to one visit, one letter and one parcel per week; and full restoration of remission lost through the protest
c: The right not to wear a prison uniform; the right not to do prison work; the right to free association with other prisoners and to organise educational and recreational pursuits; the right to   unlimited visits, one letter and one parcel per week; and full restoration of remission lost through the protest
d: The right not to wear a prison uniform; the right not to do prison work; the right to free association with other prisoners and to organise educational and recreational pursuits; the right to one visit, free letters and parcels each week; and full restoration of remission lost through the protest

Q391: The second hunger strike was famously led by Bobby Sands. When did it begin?
a: 1980
b: 1981
c: 1982
c: 1983

Q392: The second hunger strike was called off after the deaths of many of its participants. How many prisoners died during the protest?
a: 8
b: 9
c: 10
d: 12

Q393: What is 'internment'?
a: The imprisonment or confinement of people (usually in large groups) without trial
b: The imprisonment or confinement of people (usually in large groups) prior to their trials
c: The imprisonment or confinement of people (usually in large groups), pending prosecution
d: The imprisonment or confinement of people (commonly in large groups) without reason

Q394: When was internment introduced in Northern Ireland?
a: 1969
b: 1970
c: 1971
d: 1972

Q395: What was the name of the agreement that secured, amongst other things, the early release of prisoners convicted of 'terrorist activity' on behalf of organisations who were now observing the terms of the ceasefire?
a: The Good Friday Agreement
b: The Belfast Agreement
c: The Stormont Agreement
d: All of the above three answers

Q396: The biggest prison escape in British history took place in 1983 in which Irish prison?
a: Mountjoy Prison
b: Crumlin Road Jail
c: The Maze Prison
d: Portlaoise Jail

Q397: How many prisoners escaped during the biggest prison escape in British history (detailed in Q396)?
a: 32
b: 36
c: 38
d: 42

Q398: During the post-1970s Irish Troubles, a number of en masse escapes were successfully made from various Irish prisons. How many escape attempts were made?
a: 7
b: 8
c: 9
d: 10

Q399: In which well-known prison did IRA Prisoners take part in rioting in 1979?
a: Belmarsh
b: Brixton
c: Wormwood Scrubs
d: Durham

Q400: How many prison staff were killed in Northern Ireland during the country's most recent troubles?
a: 10
b: 18
c: 24
d: 29

Q401: How many operational establishments does the Northern Ireland Prison Service currently have?
a: 2
b: 3
c: 5
d: 6

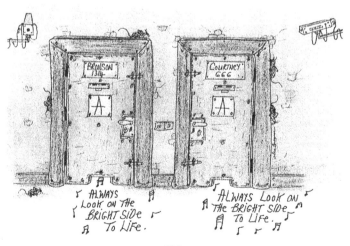

LOCATE THE PRISON

Q402: Where is HMP Altcourse located?
a: Liverpool
b: London
c: Durham
d: Buckinghamshire

Q403: Where is HMP Acklington located?
a: Newcastle
b: Evesham
c: Isle of Sheppey
d: Northumberland

Q404: Where is HMP Albany located?
a: Isle of Wight
b: Isle of Sheppey
c: Isle of Anglesey
d: Isle if Scilly

Q405: Where is HMP Askham Grange located?
a: Wales
b: Surrey
c: London
d: York

Q406: Where is HMP Aylesbury located?
a: Dartmoor
b: Buckinghamshire
c: Hertfordshire
d: Herefordshire

Q407: Where is HMP Brinsford located?
a: Wolverhampton
b: Scotland
c: Kent
d: Essex

Q408: Where is HMP Bronzfield located?
a: Liverpool
b: London
c: Middlesex
d: Buckinghamshire

Q409: Where is HMP Buckley Hall located?
a: Newcastle
b: Rochdale
c: Isle of Sheppey
d: Northumberland

Q410: Where is HMP Bulwood Hall located?
a: Wales
b: Surrey
c: London
d: Essex

Q411: Where is HMP Barlinnie located?
a: Glasgow
b: Edinburgh
c: Carlisle
d: Falkirk

Q412: Where is HMP Camp Hill located?
   a: Isle of Wight
   b: Isle of Sheppey
   c: Isle of Anglesey
   d: Isle if Scilly

Q413: Where is HMP Cookham Wood located?
   a: Newcastle
   b: Rochester
   c: Isle of Sheppey
   d: Northumberland

Q414: Where is HMP Castle Huntly located?
   a: Dundee
   b: Dundalk
   c: Devon
   d: Derbyshire

Q415: Where is HMP Cornton Vale located?
   a: Sussex
   b: Surrey
   c: Stirling
   d: Sutherland

Q416: Where is HMP Downview located?
   a: Sussex
   b: Essex
   c: Surrey
   d: Middlesex

Q417: Where is HMP Ford located?
a: Brighton
b: Dover
c: Arundel
d: Southampton

Q418: Where is HMP Forest Bank located?
a: Salford
b: Wigan
c: Bolton
d: Nottingham

Q419: Where is HMP Frankland located?
a: Durham
b: Newcastle
c: Brasside
d: Washington

Q420: Where is HMP Full Sutton located?
a: Yorkshire
b: Lancashire
c: Merseyside
d: Manchester

Q421: Where is HMP Parc located?
a: Bridgend
b: Swansea
c: Cardiff
d: Usk

Q422: Where is HMP Glenn Parva located?
    a: Luton
    b: Nottingham
    c: Leicester
    d: Falkirk

Q423: Where is HMP Dovegate located?
    a: Uttoxeter
    b: Southampton
    c: Salford
    d: Exeter

Q424: Where is HMP Hollesley Bay located?
    a: Sussex
    b: Suffolk
    c: Surrey
    d: Cornwall

Q425: Where is HMP Kirklevington Grange located?
    a: Sheffield
    b: North Yorkshire
    c: South Yorkshire
    d: Blackpool

Q426: Where is HMP Lindholme located?
    a: Glamorgan
    b: Durham
    c: Doncaster
    d: Derby

Q427: Where is HMP Long Lartin located?
   a: Everton
   b: Hereford
   c: Birmingham
   d: Evesham

Q428: Where is HMP Low Newton located?
   a: Bedford
   b: Brasside
   c: Teeside
   d: Brookside

Q429: Where is HMP Mount located?
   a: Hertfordshire
   b: Herefordshire
   c: Hampshire
   d: Derbyshire

Q430: Where is HMP North Sea Camp located?
   a: Lancashire
   b: Yorkshire
   c: Lincolnshire
   d: Scarborough

Q431: Where is HMP Northallerton located?
   a: Northampton
   b: Norwich
   c: Yorkshire
   d: Scotland

Q432: Where is HMP Onley located?
   a: Cambridge
   b: Rugby
   c: Winchester
   d: Warminster

Q433: Where is HMP Parkhurst located?
   a: Isle of Wight
   b: Isle of Man
   c: London
   d: Southampton

Q434: Where is HMP Send located?
   a: Surrey
   b: Cornwall
   c: Exeter
   d: Hampshire

Q435: Where is HMP Stocken located?
   a: Peterborough
   b: Rutland
   c: Lincolnshire
   d: Leicestershire

Q436: Where is HMP Styal located?
   a: Manchester
   b: Liverpool
   c: Cheshire
   d: Staffordshire

Q437: Where is HMP Thorn Cross located?
    a: Cheshire
    b: Hampshire
    c: Worcestershire
    d: Oxfordshire

Q438: Where is HMP Verne located?
    a: Devon
    b: Cornwall
    c: Dorset
    d: Somerset

Q439: Where is HMP Wayland located?
    a: Norfolk
    b: Norwich
    c: Ipswich
    d: Bedford

Q440: Where is HMP Wealstun located?
    a: North Yorkshire
    b: East Yorkshire
    c: South Yorkshire
    d: West Yorkshire

Q441: Where is HMP Elmley located?
    a: Northampton
    b: Norwich
    c: Kent
    d: Scotland

Q442: Where is HMP Weare located?
  a: Cambridge
  b: Portland
  c: Winchester
  d: Warminster

Q443: Where is HMP Whitemoor located?
  a: Isle of Wight
  b: Dartmoor
  c: London
  d: Cambridgeshire

Q444: Where is HMP Wolds located?
  a: Yorkshire
  b: Southampton
  c: Salford
  d: Exeter

Q445: Where is HMP Standford Hill located?
  a: Sussex
  b: Suffolk
  c: Surrey
  d: Isle of Sheppey

Q446: Where is HMP Woodhill located?
  a: Bedford
  b: Milton Keynes
  c: Luton
  d: Blackpool

Q447: Where is HMP Wormwood Scrubs located?
a: West London
b: South London
c: North London
d: Essex

Q448: Where is HMP Belmarsh located?
a: Greenwich
b: Thamesmead
c: Middlesex
d: Charlton

Q449: Where is HMP Swaleside located?
a: Newcastle
b: Rochdale
c: Isle of Sheppey
d: Northumberland

Q450: Where is HMP Pentonville located?
a: Newcastle
b: Rochester
c: Isle of Sheppey
d: North London

Do You REALLY WANNA MESS WITH Me.

ANSWERS

THE EARLY DAYS OF CRIME AND PUNISHMENT

Q1: c: The Romans introduced the first formal legal system in Britain. The laws were made by the government and enforced by the army. The Anglo Saxons used their family and friends to protect them and punish wrongdoers, and if someone broke the law it was seen as a crime against the whole community.

Later, village councils enforced punishment with 'trial by ordeal': each party argued their case in front of the council and, if the two sides could not agree, the council would 'let God decide'. This meant the accused had to carry out tasks such as carrying a red-hot iron a few paces or picking a stone out of a pan of boiling water, and if the burns did not heal within three days, the person was found guilty.

Q2: a: Hue and Cry. During the Middle Ages, the main method of catching lawbreakers was raising a 'hue and cry' when someone was seen committing a crime. All men would then give chase to catch the criminal and bring them to trial before the court. (Punishments ranged from hanging and mutilation to whipping and fining!) Any accused person could seek sanctuary within the church and many felons would ask to be tried by a church court. The ability to recite a particular psalm would often qualify a person as a cleric, and this meant they could only be tried by the church.

Q3: d: William the Conqueror. He originally built a stockade building on the site in 1066, as he was nervous about London's mobs. The stockade was replaced twenty years later when the White Tower was erected. This is the main central building that stands today.

Q4: c: The Water Gate. The name of the Water Gate was changed to 'Traitor's Gate' because it was used as the entrance to The Tower for its many famous prisoners.

Q5: b: 3 - Anne Boleyn, Catherine Howard, and Lady Jane Grey. They were all beheaded on a scaffold between Tower Green and the Chapel. Elizabeth I's alleged suitor, Robert Devereaux, Earl of Essex, was also executed here. Today there is a plaque by the site of the scaffold that lists the names of the people beheaded there.

Q6: b: St Paul's. This was originally one of the gatehouses to the city, which also served as a prison and provided a second income for the gatekeeper.

Q7: c: Newgate. It has had four different incarnations in total. The fourth was built in 1770 and was a foreboding and dreadful place, vast in size but riddled with disease.

Q8: b: Henry II. In 1176, he ordered his Sheriffs build jails in every county. Imprisonment soon became standard punishment for crimes such as vagrancy, poaching and debt; and, by Tudor times, most towns and cities had their own prisons and every county had a jail controlled by the local sheriffs.

Q9: c: Whittington's Newgate. This was the third Newgate building designed as state-of-the-art; but, despite the good intentions, the jail soon became as dreadful as it's predecessors. Corruption was rife, and such practices as applying Iron Fetters to prisoners for a fee and then removing them for another fee was a common occurrence, providing gaolers with a nice income.

Q10: True. These small prisons were often called 'Bread Compters' or 'Chicken Compters' due to their location in the city where bread or poultry was traded. These prisons where rife with corruption and neglect, and usually housed prisoners serving time for 'crimes' of debt. Being privately-run, their regimes were geared towards making profit for their owners and gaolers.

Q11: c: The Fleet. This prison was attacked by the Gordon rioters. However, rioting was different in the 18th century, and the rioters had the courtesy to send the Prison Governor a note warning him of their attack!

Q12: d: Wapping. A special set of gallows was erected at the exact point of the low water mark because the Admiralty's jurisdiction at that time was over all crimes committed in the area up to the low water mark. Also, the bodies were not cut down immediately after hanging (like those of civil executions) but were left to hang until three tides had washed over them.

Q13: c: The Houses of Parliament. A single room is located in the lower part of the clock tower, and is classed as a state prison (as are Pentonville and Wormwood Scrubs).

Q14: d: They were all prison reformists. John Howard's campaigns included a petition against the 'discharge fee' - the release fee to be paid by prisoners after completing their sentence, buying them permission to leave the gaol. As most could not afford this fee, most never got released. Today, one of the largest prison reform organisations is named after John Howard: 'The Howard Reform Trust'.

Q15: b Hulks. The ships were intended as temporary emergency measures to ease prison overcrowding by holding a small number of prisoners for short periods. However, one record describes a Hulk that held 700 prisoners with only one warder during the night shift.

Q16: b Brixton. The design for Brixton Prison was completed in 1819.

Q17: False: It was designed as a state-of-the-art prison, but turned out to be a disaster. Its modern, octagonal design meant so many twists and turns in the corridors that the warders had to mark the walls with chalk to find their way around. Also, the lack of airflow and numerous damp corners turned the atmosphere putrid and, as a result, disease flourished.

Q18: b: The Clink. This prison was owned by the Bishop of Winchester and held prisoners from the 1100's to 1780, when it was destroyed by fire by the Gordon rioters.

Q19: b: Pentonville. Prisoners here were subject to a very harsh regime, and sentences were often considerably lengthened for trivial reasons. One way to escape this uncertain future was to earn a ticket to the Australian penal colonies by volunteering to work. This is probably where we get the expression "work your ticket".

Q20: a: Between 1787 and 1868, around 164,000 people were transported to Australia. The last convict ship, the Hougoumont, left Britain in 1867 and arrived in Western Australia on January 10 1868.

Q21: b: North America. The British used North America (most notably, the Province of Georgia) as a penal colony. Convicts would be transported by private sector merchants, and auctioned off to plantation owners upon arrival. It is estimated that some 60,000 British convicts were sent to colonial America; representing, perhaps, a quarter of all

British emigrants during the eighteenth century.

Q22: b: Lady Juliana. A ship weighing 401 tonnes, she was chartered to transport prostitutes (hence her nickname, 'The Floating Brothel'). Her master was Thomas Edgar, who had sailed with James Cook on his last voyage. The surgeon was Richard Alley, who was apparently competent by the standards of the day, but made little attempt to maintain discipline. After a delay of six months, the Lady Juliana left Plymouth on July 29 1789 with 226 female convicts, and took 309 days to reach Port Jackson - one of the slowest journeys made by a convict ship.

Q23: c: The Old Bailey. The original medieval court was located on the western wall of the City of London, but destroyed in the 1666 Fire of London. It was rebuilt in 1674, with the court open to the weather to prevent the spread of disease. In 1734, it was refronted, enclosing the court and reducing the influence of spectators. This led to outbreaks of typhus - notably in 1750, when 60 people died, including the Lord Mayor and two Judges. It was rebuilt again in 1774, and a second courtroom added in 1824. A decade later, it was renamed as the Central Criminal Court and its jurisdiction extended.

Q24: False. Her Majesty's Court of Appeal is the second most senior court in the English legal system, with only the Appellate Committee of the House of Lords above it. The Court is divided into two divisions: the Civil Division and the Criminal Division. The Master of the Rolls presides over the Civil Division, and the Lord Chief Justice over the Criminal Division. The other permanent Judges of the Court of Appeal are each known as 'Lord Justice of Appeal'.

Q25: a: The Recorder of London. All judges sitting in the Old Bailey are, unusually, addressed as 'My Lord' or 'My Lady', whether they be High Court, circuit Judges or Recorders. The Lord Mayor of London and Aldermen of the City of London are entitled to sit on the Judges' bench during a hearing, but do not actively participate in trials. The most senior permanent judge of the Central Criminal Court has the title of 'the Recorder of London', and his deputy is 'Common Serjeant of London'. The present Recorder of London is His Honour Judge Peter Beaumont QC, who was appointed in December 2004, following the death earlier that year of his predecessor, His Honour Judge Michael Hyam. The present Common Serjeant is His Honour Judge Brian Barker QC.

The position of Recorder of London should not be confused with that of 'Recorder', which is the name given to lawyers who sit part-time as Crown Court Judges. A select number of the most senior criminal lawyers in the country sit at Recorders in the Central Criminal Court.

Q26: c: Typhus. Typhus was common in prisons because, in the crowded conditions, the lice that carry the bacteria by feeding on infected persons spread easily; hence, typhus became known as 'Gaol fever' or 'Jail fever'. Gaol fever often occurs when prisoners are frequently huddled together in dark, filthy rooms. In these conditions, imprisonment until the next term of court was often equivalent to a death sentence.

Typhus was so infectious that prisoners brought before the court sometimes infected members of the court. Following the Assize at Oxford in 1577 (later deemed 'the Black Assize'), over 300 died from epidemic typhus - including Sir Robert Bell, Lord Chief Baron of the Exchequer. The outbreak that followed (between 1557 and '59) killed about 10% of the English population.

During the 1730 Lent Assize Court held at Taunton, typhus caused the deaths of the Lord Chief Baron, the High Sheriff, the sergeant and hundreds of others. During a time when there were 241 capital offences, more prisoners died from 'gaol fever' than were put to death by all the public executioners in the realm. In 1759, an English authority estimated that, each year, a quarter of prisoners had died from Gaol fever In London.

Typhus frequently broke out amongst the ill-kept prisoners of Newgate Gaol, before moving in to the general city population.

Q27: b: Clerkenwell. The prison closed in 1885, the site was transferred to the Post Office in 1889 and its buildings were gradually replaced. The last sections were demolished in 1929 to make way for an extension of the Letter Office. Today, the site is occupied by the Mount Pleasant Sorting Office.

Q28: a: Coldbath Fields Prison. Coldbath Fields Prison took its name from its historic location in the fields near an important well, or medicinal spring. The prison was rebuilt in 1794, and extended in 1850.

Coldbath Fields Prison was originally the Middlesex House of Correction: a prison run by local magistrates, where most prisoners served short sentences. Until 1850, the prison housed men, women and children; thereafter it was restricted to male offenders over the age of 17. Despite its aspirations to be a more humanitarian prison (it was designed by John Howard), it became notorious for its strict regime of silence and use of the treadmill.

ENGLISH LITERATURE IN PRISON

Q29: c: Bedford

Q30: d: Reading

Q31: a: The Prisoner of Zenda. An adventure novel by Anthony Hope, published in 1894, it tells the story of a man who must impersonate a King, whom he resembles, when the king is abducted by enemies on the eve of his coronation.

Q32: d: De profundis. Psalm 130 (129 in the traditional Vulgate numbering) begins, "De profundis clamavi ad te, Domine: Domine, exaudi vocem meam" ("Out of the depths have I cried unto thee, O Lord: Lord, hear my voice"). It is in this work that Wilde describes his association with the more dubious elements of the 1890s London as "feasting with panthers".

Q33: d: Ludwig Wittgenstein. "Wovon man nicht sprechen kann, darüber muß man schweigen" ("What one cannot speak about, one must keep silent about") is one of Wittgenstein's best known sentences. (For me, Wittgenstein's works fall into that category!)

Q34: c: Fanny Hill. Criminal prosecutions of literary works had hitherto tended to concentrate on alleged blasphemy and sedition; but, by George II's time, the authorities were giving more attention to alleged obscenity. Cleland was summoned before the Privy Council soon after the book was published, but was not punished. However, in 1757, a bookseller named Drybutter was prosecuted and pilloried for selling a version of the work; and for the next 200 years or so, publishers and sellers of the book were prosecuted and convicted. The last notable conviction was that of paperback publishers, Mayflower Books, in 1964. Public opinion was rapidly changing, however: six years later, Mayflower published the book again, and were not prosecuted
(It is interesting to note that the name of the Home Office HQ in London is Cleland House!)

Q35: b: Thomas Paine. Having attacked the British political system in 'The Rights of Man', Paine then turned his attention to religion in 'The Age of Reason'. Paine was not an atheist, but he could not stomach orthodox Christianity, finding the Old Testament to consist of "obscene stories and voluptuous debaucheries", and the New Testament to be inconsistent and self-contradictory. English publishers and booksellers that sold the work were prosecuted for blasphemous libel (a common-law offence which still exists in England in 2006).

Q36: d: Richard Lovelace. Lovelace, the son and heir of a wealthy Kentish landowner, served a short spell in the Gatehouse in

Westminster in 1642, after presenting to Parliament the 'Kentish petition' that called for the restoration of the King's rights. The Anglican liturgy, 'To Althea', is believed to have been written then, although this cannot be proved.

Q37: c: Thomas Malory. Malory is usually identified as Sir Thomas Malory of Newbold Revel in Warwickshire. He became a knight in 1442 and a Member of Parliament in 1445. He spent most of the 1450s in prison on charges including murder, robbery and rape, though he does not seem to have been brought to trial and was released on bail more than once. His synthesis of the Arthurian legends is the source of most of the later Arthurian literature in the English-speaking world. The fact that he spent such a long time in prison and was linked with Newbold Revel is ironic, as Newbold Revel is now used as a training college for new entrant Prison Officers.

Q38: b: Robinson Crusoe. Defoe was jailed on August 3 1703 for distributing pamphlets that promoted the work of Dissenters (those who had separated from the Church of England). Dissenters opposed state interference in religious matters; and, from the 16th to the 18th century, founded their own communities.

Q39: d: Thomas More. More was beheaded in 1535 after more than a year in the Tower. His 'Dialogue' recommends a kind of Christian stoicism in the face of adversity and death, and contains a fairly lengthy consideration of the rights and wrongs of suicide.

Q40: d: Sir Walter Raleigh. Raleigh spent some twelve and a half years in prison for allegedly conspiring against the King. He was eventually beheaded, after being released "under peril of law" to lead an abortive expedition to South America. His 'History' deals with Egyptian, Greek and biblical history from 168 BC/BCE.

Q41: a: A Tale of Two Cities. In Dickens' novel, 'A Tale of Two Cities', the Old Bailey is the courthouse where Charles Darnay is put on trial for treason.

Q42: b: 1777. Amongst his many proposals, John Howard suggested that gaolers should not be allowed to charge prisoners for 'luxury' items such as beds, food, removing iron fetters and shackles, etc. He also proposed that steps be taken to make prisons healthier and disease-free environments. The Act to prevent gaolers from charging prisoners was not passed until nearly forty years later, in 1815.

Q43: a: William Thomas Stead. In 1885, he entered into a crusade against child prostitution, publishing a series of articles entitled 'The Maiden Tribute of Modern Babylon'. In order to demonstrate the truth of his revelations, he arranged the 'purchase' of the thirteen-year old daughter of a chimney sweep, Eliza Armstrong. Though his action is thought to have aided the passing of the Criminal Law Amendment Act of 1885, it made his position on the paper impossible. In fact, it led to his conviction and three-month term of imprisonment at Coldbath Fields and Holloway, convicted on grounds that he had secured permission only from the mother (and not the father) for 'purchase' of the girl. (Had he secured both parents' permission, the 'transaction' would have been legal.)

In April 1912, Stead boarded the RMS Titanic for a visit to America to take part in a peace congress. After the ship struck the iceberg, Stead helped several women and children into the lifeboats and, after all the boats had gone, went into the 1st Class Smoking Room and was last seen sitting in a leather chair and reading a book.

Q44: b: Landsberg Prison. On November 8 1923, Hitler and the SA stormed a public meeting headed by Kahr in the Bürgerbräukeller, a large beer hall outside of Munich. He declared that he had set up a new government with Ludendorff and demanded, at gunpoint, the support of Kahr and the local military establishment for the destruction of the Berlin government. He was soon arrested for high treason and Alfred Rosenberg became temporary leader of the party. During Hitler's trial, he was given almost unlimited time to speak, and his popularity soared as he voiced nationalistic sentiments. A Munich personality became a nationally-known figure. On April 1 1924, Hitler was sentenced to five years' imprisonment at Landsberg Prison, where he received favoured treatment from the guards and much fan mail from admirers. He was pardoned and released from jail in December 1924, as part of a general amnesty for political prisoners, having served nine months of his sentence (just over a year, including time on remand).

While at Landsberg, he dictated 'Mein Kampf' ('My Struggle', originally entitled 'Four Years of Struggle against Lies, Stupidity, and Cowardice') to his deputy, Rudolf Hess. The book - dedicated to Thule Society member, Dietrich Eckart - was an autobiography and exposition of his ideology. It was published in two volumes in 1925 and 1926, selling about 240,000 copies between 1925 and 1934. By the end of the war, about 10 million copies had been sold or distributed (newly-weds and soldiers received free copies).

Q45: a: Klong Prem Prison. In August 1996, Englishman David McMillan escaped from Thailand's Klong Prem Prison (sometimes called 'the

Bangkok Hilton') while awaiting trial on drug charges. McMillan cut the bars of his shared cell, scaled four walls, dropped over the electrified outer wall using a bamboo ladder, and then skirted the moat while hiding his face under an umbrella from the prison factory. The breakout was described in 'Escape', published in 2007.

Q46: a: June and Jennifer Gibbons. The twin sisters were inseparable and had speech impediments that made it difficult for people outside their immediate family to understand them. They did not mix a great deal with other children and, when they turned 14 and a succession of therapists had tried unsuccessfully to get them to communicate with others, they were sent to separate boarding schools in an attempt to break their isolation. This was a disaster: the pair became catatonic and entirely withdrawn when parted. When they were re-united, the two spent a couple of years isolating themselves in their bedroom, engaged in elaborate play with dolls. They created many plays and stories in a soap-opera style, reading some of them aloud on tape as gifts for their little sister. Inspired by a pair of gift diaries at Christmas 1979, they began their writing careers, and each wrote several novels. Desperate for recognition and fame (and perhaps publicity for their books), the girls committed a number of petty crimes; including arson, which led to their being committed to Broadmoor Hospital. They remained there for fourteen years. Within hours after their release in 1993, Jennifer died of sudden inflammation of the heart (reported initially as viral myocarditis). There was no evidence of drugs or poison in her system, and, to this day, Jennifer's death remains a mystery. After Jennifer's death, June gave interviews with Harper's Bazaar and The Guardian, becoming more communicative and able to speak to other people.

HISTORICAL FIGURES IN PRISON

Q47: b: The Bloody Tower. While Raleigh was imprisoned, he was permitted to conduct scientific experiments; and is traditionally credited with distilling freshwater from saltwater. While there, he also wrote his 'History of the World', published in 1614 - just four years before he was beheaded at Westminster.

Q48: b: Mary Queen of Scots

Q49: a: Thomas Parker. In 1716, Thomas Parker became Lord Chancellor, was given a pension for life, and became a favourite of the King. In 1718, he was advanced to the title of Earl of Macclesfield, with the additional subsidiary title of Viscount Parker. In 1721, he was implicated in financial irregularities, though he did not resign as Lord Chancellor until 1724. The following year, he was impeached and tried in the House of Lords. He was unanimously found guilty of corruption for taking more than £100,000 in bribes (more than £11million in today's currency). He was struck off the roll of the Privy Council, fined £30,000 and placed in the Tower of London until payment was received. He had been a fabulously wealthy man (possibly due to his corruption) but, as this money was now confiscated, he had no resources with which to pay his fine, and consequently spent most of the rest of his life at Shirburn Castle, where he was buried.

Q50: c: The Marshalsea. Dickens visited this prison many times, and set his novel 'Little Dorrit' here: a prison notorious for the cruelty of its regime.

Q51: a: Newgate. Kidd was held at Newgate before being tried without representation, where he was shocked to learn (only at his trial) that he was charged with murder. He was found guilty on all charges (murder and five counts of piracy) and hanged on May 23 1701, at 'Execution Dock', Wapping, London. During the execution, the hangman's rope broke and Kidd was hanged on the second attempt.

Q52: b: Tower of London. Despite its apparent macabre history, very few people were actually executed at the tower. Fawkes himself was actually hung, drawn and quartered at Old Palace Yard in Westminister.

Q53: b: 'The Man in The Iron Mask' was kept in the Bastille in France.

Q54: a: Mary Wade. Mary Wade was only 11 years old when transported to Australia: the youngest convict aboard the Lady Juliana. Mary spent her days sweeping the streets of London as a means of begging, being one of a large family with a single mother, living in poverty. With another child, said to be 14 years old, Mary stole the clothes off a small 8 year old girl and pawned them. However, young Mary was turned in by yet another child, and arrested. She was brought before the court on January 14 1789, where she was sentenced to death. On March 11 1789, King George III was proclaimed cured of an unnamed madness (it is assumed that he suffered from porphyria, a degenerative mental disease). Five days later, in the spirit of celebration, all women on death row (including Mary Wade) had their sentences commuted to transportation. Mary spent 93 days in Newgate Prison, before being transported on the 'Lady Juliana' (the first convict ship to hold only women and children) for an 11 month voyage across the ocean to Sydney, where she arrived on June 3 1790. She was then sent on to

Norfolk Island (on the 'Surprize') arriving on August 7 1790.

Q55: c: Jonathan Wild. Jonathan Wild (baptised May 6 1683, died May 24 1725) was perhaps the most famous criminal in London — and possibly Great Britain — during the 18th century, because of both his own actions and the uses novelists, playwrights and political satirists made of them. He invented a scheme that allowed him to run one of the most successful gangs of thieves of the era, whilst appearing to be the nation's leading policeman. He manipulated the press and the nation's fears to become the most loved public figure of the 1720s; but this love, of course, turned to hatred when his villainy was exposed. After his death, he became a symbol of corruption and hypocrisy.

Q56: d: 4. He was arrested and imprisoned five times in 1724, but managed to escape four times, making him a notorious public figure, wildly popular with the poorer classes. Ultimately, he was caught, convicted and hanged at Tyburn, ending his criminal career after less than two years.

Q57: a: William Palmer, a poisoner and murderer. The Court was originally for trial of only those crimes committed in the capital, but in 1856, public revulsion at the accusations made against doctor William Palmer led to fears that he could not enjoy a fair trial in his native Staffordshire. The Central Criminal Court Act 1856 was passed to enable his trial at the Old Bailey.

Q58: a: Roderick McLean. Roderick McLean attempted to assassinate Queen Victoria with a pistol on March 2 1882 at Windsor. This was the last of six attempts over a period of forty years to kill or assault Victoria, and it was the only one in which the gun in use was actually loaded. (McLean's motive was purportedly revenge for a curt reply to poetry of his mailed to the Queen.) Tried for high treason on April 20, the jury took five minutes to find the Scotsman "not guilty, but insane". He lived out his remaining days in Broadmoor Asylum.

The verdict prompted the Queen to ask for a change in English law so that those implicated in future cases with similar outcomes would be considered "guilty, but insane".

Q59: a: Harry Jackson. On June 27 1902, a burglary occurred in a house in Denmark Hill, London, and some billiard balls were stolen. The investigating officer noticed a number of fingerprints on a freshly painted windowsill, apparently where the burglar made his entry. He immediately called the Metropolitan Police Fingerprint Bureau, and Detective-Sergeant Charles Stockley Collins went to the scene. He examined the marks and decided that the left thumb made the clearest impression. Returning to the Bureau, Collins and his colleagues made a search of their files for known criminals with a similar print pattern. The files revealed that the fingerprints belonged to a 41-year old labourer, Harry Jackson, who had recently served a prison term for burglary. He was arrested and - for safety's sake - fingerprinted again. This new set was compared to the prints photographed from the crime scene and, again, they matched. When Harry Jackson went on trial at the Old Bailey, Muir convinced the jury of the absolute reliability of fingerprint evidence. As a result, Harry Jackson was found guilty and sentenced to seven years in prison on September 13 1902.

Q60: a: Dr Crippen. Dr Hawley Harvey Crippen was hanged in Pentonville, England, on November 23 1910 for murdering his wife. He has gone down in history as the first criminal to be captured with the aid of wireless communication.

Q61: a: Tower of London. Rudolf Hess, deputy leader of the German Nazi Party, was the last state prisoner to be held in the tower. In May 1941, he was arrested after parachuting into Scotland, apparently on a peace mission. He was imprisoned in the Tower for a few days, before being released to take part in secret talks. During the Second World War, the Tower was used to hold many German POWs; in particular, captured members of German U boat crews.

Q62: Rudolf Hess passed away in Spandau Prison in 1987. He was 93 years old, making him the oldest prisoner in the world at the time.

Q63: b: William Joyce. In late August 1939, shortly before the start of World War II, Joyce and his wife Margaret fled to Germany. Joyce had been tipped off that the British authorities intended to detain him under Defence Regulation 18B, so he became a naturalised German in 1940. He was recruited immediately for radio announcements and script writing at German radio's English service. These broadcasts urged the British people to surrender, and were well-known for their jeering, sarcastic and menacing tone. However, far from breaking British morale, they served only to increase either resentment or ridicule of Joyce.

Q64: a: Wandsworth. Lord Haw Haw was executed on January 3 1946, at Wandsworth Prison, aged 39. He was the second-to-last person to be hanged for a crime other than murder in the United Kingdom. The last was Theodore Schurch, who was executed the following day at Pentonville. In both cases the hangman was Albert Pierrepoint.

Q65: c: Theodore Schurch. On July 8 1936, Schurch enlisted in the British Army as a Royal Army Service Corps driver. In June 1942, Schurch was captured by the Germans in Tobruk and began a career working for both Italian and German intelligence. Often he would pose as a captured prisoner-of-war to gain the trust of fellow Allied prisoners, and one of his 'victims' was Colonel Sir David Stirling, founder of the Special Air Service. Schurch was arrested in Rome, in March 1945, and tried by a court martial convened at the Duke of York's Headquarters in Chelsea, London. In September 1945, he was found guilty of all ten charges against him: nine counts of treachery under section one of the Treachery Act 1940, and one charge of desertion. Theodore Schurch was hanged on January 4 1946 at the age of 27. His hanging took place at HMP Pentonville, and was conducted by Albert Pierrepoint. Schurch was the only British soldier executed for treachery in the Second World War

Q66: c: George Blake. In 1953, Blake was sent by MI6 to work as an agent in Berlin, where he made contact with the KGB and informed them of the details of British and US operations and betrayed hundreds of MI6 agents. Two notable incidents in which he was involved were the Berlin Tunnel and the Boris affair.

Q67: b: 42. The maximum sentence for treason was 14 years, but the Crown wanted more. His activities were divided into three time periods and, in 1961 - after an on-camera trial, he was sentenced to 14 years on each of three three counts of treason - 42 years in total - by the Lord Chief Justice, Lord Parker of Waddington. This sentence was said, by newspapers, to represent one year for each of the agents killed when he betrayed them; although this claim appears to be an invention. It was, at that time, the longest sentence ever handed down by a British court.

Q68: a: Wormwood Scrubs. Blake escaped from Wormwood Scrubs and fled to the USSR, where he divorced his wife (with whom he had three children) and started a new life. In 1990, he published his autobiography. He is still living in Moscow, Russia, on a KGB pension, and remains a committed Marxist-Leninist. Blake denied being a traitor, insisting that he had never felt British: "To betray, you first have to belong. I never belonged".

Q69: d: The KGB, IRA and the British Security Services. He escaped from prison with the help of Pat Pottle, Michael Randle and Sean Bourke. Bourke, an Irishman, was serving 7 years for sending a bomb to a senior policeman. Randle and Pottle were founder members of the Committee of 100, an anti-nuclear direct action group, and describe themselves as libertarians and 'quasi-anarchists'. For 22 years, the details of the escape remained a secret. Common wisdom held that it must have been a professional operation, masterminded by the KGB, the Provisional Irish Republican Army or even the British security services. As Michael Randle said: "It was to be an entirely unprofessional – almost, one could say, DIY – affair".

Q70: c: Alfie Hinds. Hinds escaped from Nottingham Prison after sneaking through the locked doors and over a 20-foot prison wall, for which he became known in the press as 'Houdini Hinds'. He spent eight months as a fugitive, working as a builder-decorator in Ireland and throughout Europe, until his arrest by Scotland Yard detectives in 1956. Hinds also escaped from the Law Courts in Fleet Street, and later from Chelmsford Prison. His notorious jail breaks from three high security prisons (and his successful libel case) earned Hinds celebrity status, and he soon became a sought-after speaker, criticising the English legal system.

Q71: a: George Davis. Davis was serving a 20-year prison sentence for the Ilford LEB robbery when, on August 19 1975, it was discovered that the pitch at the Headingley cricket ground had been dug up, preventing further play in the test match between England and Australia. This dramatic direct action protest by relatives and friends of George Davis was accompanied by campaign graffiti proclaiming "Free George Davis", "Justice for George Davis", "George Davis is Innocent". In May 1976, despite a recent Court of Appeal decision not to overturn Davis' criminal conviction, the Home Secretary, Roy Jenkins, agreed to recommend the release of Davis by Exercise of the Royal Prerogative of Mercy because of doubts over the evidence presented by the police that had helped convict him. Needless to say, this was a highly exceptional turn of events.

Q72: b: Franz Muller. Muller, a German tailor, murdered Thomas Briggs in the first murder committed on a British train. The case caught the imagination of the public, due to increasing safety fears about rail travel at the time, and Muller was pursued across the Atlantic Ocean by Scotland Yard detectives. On July 9 1864, Thomas Briggs, a city banker, was travelling on the 9:50pm North London Railway train between Fenchurch Street and Hackney Wick. He was beaten and robbed of his gold watch and gold spectacles, and his body thrown from the carriage. Despite maintaining his innocence throughout his trial, Muller confessed to the crime immediately before being hanged. His last words were reported to be, "Ich habe es gethan" ("I did it"), in response to a question as to whether he was responsible for the death of Briggs. The murder of

Briggs resulted in the establishment of compulsory communication between train passengers and members of the crew. If Briggs had been able to contact the train driver or guard, the murder could have been prevented.

THE VICTORIAN ERA

Q73: d: Wandsworth, Wormwood Scrubs, Pentonville and Brixton. These prisons have changed very little from Victorian times, and are still very foreboding places (despite the addition of brighter paint on the walls and integral sanitation).

Q74: d: Prisoners built Wormwood Scrubs. They completed the prison Chapel first (to give themselves a place to worship), and all the tools used in the construction were made by prisoners in other prisons around the country.

Q75: c: Suffragettes. The suffragette movement campaigned for the right of women to vote. Their direct political action became more and more public, and many protestors were arrested and imprisoned. Other protestors deliberately sought to get themselves imprisoned, in order to fill the prisons to capacity. On one day in 1907, Holloway took delivery of 75 suffragettes. The fight for suffrage proved to be a long one, as it was not until 1918 that women (and even then, only those over the age of 30 who married, graduates, owners of property and householders) were finally granted the right to vote.

Q76: d: The Convict Service. This was established to give the Secretary of State the authority to appoint Directors of Prisons to take over the management of both the Hulks and the Prisons.

Q77: c: The Prisons Act. This Act was passed in 1878 and brought all prisons under the control of a national system run by the prison commission.

Q78: True. There are many stories relating to this fact. One of the most popular is that Queen Victoria delayed the opening of the prison after inspecting it and showing her disgust at the fact that criminals could use the toilet, while her law-abiding citizens could not afford such luxuries, and ordering all the toilets be removed before the prison could officially open. The toilets were, in fact, removed in 1870 to make room in the cells for more prisoners. 'Slopping out' (using buckets in cells) was introduced, and remained the practice until 1996.

Q79: d: Wandsworth was originally named 'The Surrey House Of Correction'.

Q80: b The Napoleonic War. This war ended shortly after construction finished, and the prison was used to house prisoners from the new war in America.

Q81: c: American

Q82: d: 1869

Q83: c: New Bailey Prison. Strangeways was built to replace the New Bailey Prison in Salford, which closed in 1868.

Q84: c: 1902

Q85: c: Rochester. The first youth institution was established near Rochester at Borstal Prison, in the small village of Borstal, near Rochester, Kent.

Q86: c: Hard bed, board and labour. In the latter part of the 19th century - after the 1865 Prisons Act, and under Assistant Director of Prisons, Sir Edmund du Cane - prison life was made even tougher. Hard plank beds replaced hammocks, food was deliberately boring and inmates had to work hard on monotonous (even pointless) tasks.

Q87: a: One year in solitary, followed by three years hard labour. To bring prisons further into line, they were all taken out of local control in 1877, and taken under government control, by the Home Office. The old, small prisons were shut down. By this time, the normal sentence was one year in solitary confinement, followed by three years hard labour. Even time off for good behaviour was stopped, and corporal punishment (whipping) continued.

Q88: b: Cherry Hill. The 'separate system', based on Cherry Hill Prison in Pennsylvania, USA, was where prisoners were kept in solitary confinement in order to have them think about their life and crimes. It was believed that they would then come to understand the error of their ways. The Chaplain played an important part in this, encouraging prisoners to turn to religion. Even when taking exercise or in chapel, prisoners could not see or talk to each other.

Q89: d: Pentonville. Pentonville opened in 1842 under the separate system. Shortly afterwards, several of its prisoners went mad, and three committed suicide.

Q90: a: Auburn. Under the 'silent system', based on Auburn Prison, New York, USA, prisoners could work, but it had to be monotonous and pointless work, done in total silence. The work included the infamous treadmill: a large wheel on which prisoners walked, sometimes to drive a mill, and sometimes just to create work. Another form of 'work' was 'the crank': a large handle located in each cell, with a counter, which the prisoner had to turn so-many-thousand times a day. (Warders could tighten up the crank, if they wished, making it harder to turn: hence their nickname "screws".) There was also 'shot drill', which meant passing cannon-balls one to another along a line. The work was intended to be hard and degrading, in order to break the prisoners' will and self-respect.

Q91: c: Separating old bits of rope strands. 'Picking oakum' was the name given to separating the strands of old ropes so that they could be used again. (This is where the saying 'money for old rope' comes from.)

EXECUTIONS IN PRISON

Q92: a: Suspension hanging, short drop, standard drop and long drop. These were the four methods of performing a judicial hanging. A mechanised form of hanging - the upright jerker - was also experimented with in the 19th century.

Q93: a: 7. Despite its dark myths and legends, only seven prisoners were ever actually beheaded at the Tower for treason. Five of these were women.

Q94: b: Tyburn. Some 50,000 criminals met their death at the gallows in Tyburn, before the execution site was relocated to Newgate in 1783. A plaque now marks the site of the Tyburn gallows at the junction of Oxford Street and Edgware Road.

Q95: b: Pentonville. This was the site of the first 'execution shed' and inherited the gallows beam from the public execution site at Newgate.

Q96: a: Pentonville 17th June 1954. Britain's last double (side-by-side) hanging took place at Pentonville on Thursday 17 June 1954, when 22-year-old Kenneth Gilbert and 24-year-old Ian Grant were executed by Albert Pierrepoint (assisted by Royston Rickard, Harry Smith and Joe Broadbent) for the murder of 55-year-old George Smart in the course of a robbery. George Smart was the hotel night porter at Aban Court Hotel in Kensington, and on the night of Tuesday 9 March, caught these two young men breaking into the hotel. They attacked him, tied him up and gagged him, ultimately causing his death by asphyxia. They blamed each other at their trial, and assured the jury that they had not intended to kill Mr Smart. The jury was not impressed with this argument - and nor was Lord Goddard, when he dismissed their subsequent appeal. They had stolen just £2 and a quantity of cigarettes – hardly worth dying for!

Q97: d: Double hangings were outlawed by the Homicide Act of 1957.

Q98: b: 120

Q99: b: Irma Grese. Grese and eleven others were convicted of crimes committed at both Auschwitz and Belsen, and sentenced to death. Her subsequent appeal was rejected. The other eleven included two other women, Juana Bormann and Elisabeth Volkenrath. On December 13 1945,, in Hameln Jail, Grese was led to the gallows and hanged by noted British executioner Albert Pierrepoint, assisted by Regimental Sergeant-Major O'Neill. She was the youngest woman to die judicially under English law in the 20th century, aged 22. Her last spoken word was: "Schnell!" ("Quickly!").

Q100: b: 1953. Bentley was convicted and sentenced to death on the evidence that he apparently said, "Let him have it", to his accomplice on the November 2 1952.

Q101: a: Wandsworth. Derek Bentley was one of the last prisoners to be hung at Wandsworth Prison. He was executed on January 28 1953, by Albert Pierrepoint, aged 19.

Q102: c: 1998. Iris initially won a Royal Pardon on July 29 1993, in respect of his death sentence. Eventually - on July 30 1998, some forty five years after his execution - the Court of Appeal set aside his conviction for murder.

Q103: a: David Blakely. Ellis shot Blakely - in full public view - outside the Magdala public house in Hampstead, on Easter Sunday 1955.

Q104: d: Holloway, July 1955. Ruth Ellis was hung on July 13 1955, in Holloway prison. Ruth had an army of supporters who campaigned for her reprieve and collected 50,000 signatures on one petition alone. However, Ruth seemed to be the only one who did not object to her fate, confiding to a friend that the prospect of execution seemed no more alarming to her "than having a tooth out".

Q105: All four of these men were hangmen, and belonged to a group of hangmen who were known as 'The Usual Suspects'.

Q106: b: 435. Albert Pierrepoint was by far the most prolific British hangman of the twentieth century. In office between 1932 and 1956, he is credited with having executed 435 men and women, including 6 US soldiers at Shepton Mallet and Nazis after the Second World War. He never confirmed the precise number himself, and even declined to do so when giving testimony to the Royal Commission on Capital Punishment in 1949.

Q107: c: 17

Q108: c: 135 prisoners were hung at Wandsworth. This figure includes the only woman ever to be hung there: Kate Webster, executed in 1879 for the murder of her mistress.

Q109: c: HMP Wandsworth. The gallows were still checked weekly up until the time they were dismantled. It is rumoured that they are still in storage, ready to be reconstructed should they be needed by any future 'traitors' sentenced to the death penalty.

Q110: c: Treason against the Crown

Q111: a: HMP Walton and HMP Strangeways. Executions continued in prisons until August 13 1964, when Gwynne Owen Evans was hanged at 8:00 am at Strangeways Prison, and Peter Anthony Allen simultaneously at Walton Prison Liverpool (both for the murder - during a robbery - of John Alan West).

Q112: b: Harry Allen and Robert Leslie Stewart. Gwynne Owen Evans was hanged by executioner Harry Allen at Manchester's Strangeways Prison at 8:00 am on August 13 1964. At the same time, Peter Allen was hanged at Liverpool's Walton Prison by Robert Leslie Stewart.

Q113: c: James Hanratty. Hanratty was the eighth-to-last person to be hanged in Britain for murder. He was executed on April 4 1962, after his conviction for the notorious 1961 'A6 Murder'. The guilt of the later convicts was never in doubt, but Hanratty's has been disputed. Hanratty was a professional car thief, convicted of the murder of Michael Gregsten at Deadman's Hill on the A6 (near the village of Clophill,

Bedfordshire, on August 22 1961). Gregsten's companion, Valerie Storie was raped and shot (non-fatally), during the incident. Charges on these additional crimes were kept in reserve

The case was a cause célèbre for opponents of the death penalty, who maintained that Hanratty was innocent and sought to draw attention to evidence that cast doubt on the validity of his conviction. However, following an appeal by his family, modern testing of DNA from his exhumed corpse and members of his family convinced Court of Appeal judges in 2002 that his guilt was proved 'beyond doubt'.

FAMOUS AND INFAMOUS PRISONERS AND THEIR ASSOCIATES

Q114: b: Wandsworth. Ronnie Biggs successfully escaped from Wandsworth in 1965 by scaling the perimeter wall. He eventually fled to Brazil (via France and Australia) where he remained at large until voluntarily giving himself up on May 7 2001. During my tour of Wandsworth on my first day as a trainee Prison Officer in 1992, I was proudly shown the property box in the store that still held Ronnie's possessions and was still marked with his name and prison number.

Q115: d: Frank Mitchell, Charlie Bronson and Frank Fraser. These men were the only three people who have ever dared to walk over the brass grille. All movement is controlled in a military manner by the centre Principle Officer, and all persons must pass around the centre in a clockwise manner without speaking.

Q116: c: 3. Charlie has dared to run the grille three times in all; and, each time, he paid dearly for his few seconds of defiance with a lengthy stretch in 'the hole' and some personal readjustment therapy from the block screws.

Q117: a: Billy Hill. Hill was born into a London criminal family and began as a house burglar in the late 1920s. He later specialised in 'smash-and-grab' raids, targeting furriers and jewellers in the 1930s. During World War II, he moved into the black market, specialising in foods and gasoline and supplying forged documents for deserting servicemen. He was also involved in East End protection rackets with fellow gangster Jack Spot. In the 1940s, he was charged with burgling a warehouse; and he fled to South Africa, where he took over illegal activities in several Johannesburg nightclubs. Following an arrest for assault, he was extradited to Britain and convicted and imprisoned for the warehouse robbery. Following his release, he opened several legitimate nightclubs, while expanding his criminal activities. In 1952, he robbed a postal van and netted more than £250,000. During this period, he also ran a cigarette smuggling operation from Morocco. Towards the end of the 1950s, Hill retired from active involvement in criminal enterprises and served as a financeer for other gangsters. He continued to run his nightclubs (including one in the fashionable Sunningdale section of Surrey) into the 1970s. He died of natural causes, as a very wealthy man.

Q118: c: His involvement in the Cable Street Riots. Jack 'Spot' Comer was a notorious Jewish gangster during the 1930s, 40s and 50s. Spot was seen as somewhat of a hero as a result of his involvement in the Cable Street Riots. He and his Jewish pals heard that the Fascist leader Oswald Mosley was planning a march through the streets of the East End on Sunday 4 October 1936, creating a great deal of anger and resentment throughout the Jewish community. Spot waited until half of the 2,500 Blackshirts had passed, aiming to split the parade into two sections. After yelling, "Down with Fascism!", he and his mob charged into the fascists with full power, injuring as many Blackshirts and police as possible. Spot single-handedly knocked-out Mosley's leading minder, a Wrestler called Roughneck. After Roughneck went down, one of Spot's mobs from the other side of the street attacked the Blackshirts and soon many hundreds of ordinary Eastenders fought side-by-side: Jews and gentiles. Eventually, Spot found himself alone and was totally surrounded by coppers with batons. He put up a good fight but was badly beaten and sent to hospital - and then prison.

His involvement in the Cable Street Riots earned him the respect of the Jews and many others in the East End communities. Jack Spot went on to say, "This was more than a mob fight: It was a victory over the Nazis. I don't want to swank, but that night, I was the hero of the East End". During his time in prison, he learnt a lot from other criminals in all areas of crime and it was not long before he re-established the protection rackets, principally offering protection against the fascist Blackshirts.

Q119: c: Rang the brass bell located near the office. Never being one to do things by halves - and not content to just break the rule for a third time - Charlie decided to ring the huge brass bell located by the Principle Officers' office as loudly as possible, before being overpowered by some irate and embarrassed Prison Officers. This bell was sacred in Wandsworth, and rung only by the Centre Principle Officer to raise the alarm during an incident on one of the wings. Charlie's feet did not touch the ground after this little prank, and he found himself lying very bruised in the segregation unit for a very long time.

Q120: a: 1,790. Despite completing this phenomenal amount of sit-ups in one hour and having it recorded by legitimate physical training instructors and time keepers (myself included), the Guinness Book of Records failed to record it, stating it did not recognise medicine ball sit-ups as a registered sporting activity.

Q121: c: Frank Fraser. He spotted the country's most prolific hangman on the landing one day, obviously 'sizing' someone up for the noose, and saw an opportunity too good to be passed-up. It landed him a hefty spell in solitary, but 'the hole' was Frank's home-from-home in those days.

Q122: a: Wally Probyn. The story of their escape was so widespread that a film was about their lives, escape and subsequent recapture. McVicar was played by Who frontman, Roger Daultry, and the film became a British classic. John McVicar used the remainder of his time in prison to educate himself, and is now a very successful writer and reporter for national newspapers.

Q123: d: Broadmoor. Charlie has scaled many prison roofs in frustration and protest at his continued segregation; but, amazingly, he has managed to get on to Broadmoor roof on three separate occasions. During one rooftop protest, he held out for almost a week, surviving on a diet of birds' eggs that he found in the nests in the tiles. He only came down after falling ill, and he was later diagnosed with pleurisy. Amongst his famous sayings are: "I do love a good night on the tiles" and "I've been on more roofs than Father Christmas".

Q124: d: 42

Q125: c: 3

Q126: d: 22. Amongst the 22 prisons in which Roy 'Pretty Boy' Shaw has been incarcerated is the notorious, special high security hospital, Broadmoor.

Q127: d: A court jesters outfit. Dave Courtney appeared before justices at Bow Street, on November 8 1999, wearing a court jester's outfit, where the magistrate commented on his outfit's being "colourful". He was accompanied by four of his 'firm'; one of whom, Brendan, was clutching a shopping bag containing £50,000 in cash for bail.

Q128: a: Sid Draper and John Kendall. Both men escaped from the exercise yard at Gartree Prison. It was this daring escape that prompted the Prison Service to construct cage roofs for the exercise yards of all its high risk units. (I actually met John Kendall during my time on the special unit at Belmarsh and, as with a lot of the old school criminals, he was a real gentleman.)

Q129: d: Winchester and Parkhurst. Ronnie was certified in Winchester Prison in the 1950s, and again in Parkhurst in the 1970s.

Q130: b: Roberta

Q131: a: Bruce Reynolds, Charlie Wilson and Ronnie Biggs

Q132: d: Jack Slipper. The robbery was investigated by Detective Chief Superintendent Jack Slipper of the Metropolitan Police (widely known in the press as 'Slipper of the Yard'), who became so involved in the case that he continued to hunt down many of the escaped robbers during his retirement. He was one of those who believed Biggs should not be released after returning to the UK in 2001; and, up until the time of his death on August 24 2005 (aged 81), he often appeared in the media to comment on any news item connected to the robbery.

Q133: d: Allen Lord and Paul Taylor

Q134: d: Dave Courtney. Dave has carried out many pranks to 'buck the system' in his own special way; including appearing in court dressed as a court jester, and purchasing an official OBE from an antiques fair.

Q135: a: Valerio Viccei. Police forensic investigators discovered a fingerprint at the crimescene that was traced to Valerio. After a period of surveillance, several of his accomplices were arrested during a series of coordinated raids on August 12 1987, and later convicted of the crime. Valerio, however, fled to Latin America. Later, on his return to England to retrieve and ship his beloved Ferrari to Latin America, police arrested him. Later, out on a day-release from prison, he was shot to death by police. Taking a huge secret to the grave: where he hid his more than $95million loot. Valerio was considered a real gentleman, and I have only ever heard good things about him from all the staff and prisoners who met him.

Q136: a: Graham Young. Graham Frederick Young was a British murderer who poisoned three people to death (his stepmother, and, years later, two work colleagues - Bob Egle and Fred Biggs), as well as administering smaller doses of poison to scores of others. Young died in his cell at Parkhurst Prison in 1990, aged 42. The official cause of death was listed as a myocardial infarction, but there is some conjecture that fellow prisoners were the real culprits.

Q137: c: Bob Maudsley

Q138: c: Hull Prison

Q139: a: Parkhurst

Q140: a: Belmarsh. Charlie took the Iraqis hostage in their cell on block four in Belmarsh Prison (the block recently converted to house category A inmates). Rather ironically, the Iraqis received five years for hijacking a plane at Stanstead airport, while Charlie received seven years for taking them hostage in prison!

Q141: a: b: or c: Any two of the following will be accepted: Hugh Callaghan, Paddy Hill, Gerard Hunter, Richard McIlkenny, William Power and John Walker. These men were sentenced to life imprisonment in 1975 for two pub bombings in Birmingham the previous year that had killed twenty-one people. The men involved in this infamous miscarriage of justice were eventually released in 1991, after having their convictions overturned by the Court of Appeal. They had served sixteen years.

Q142: d: Paul Edmunds

Q143: b: Bertie Smalls. Although there have been informers throughout history, the Smalls case was significant for three reasons: he was the first informer to give the police names of his associates and provide the evidence that would send dozens of them to prison to serve long sentences; he was the first criminal informer to strike a written deal with the Director of Public Prosecutions; and he was the only criminal informer to serve no time for his crime in return for providing Queen's evidence.

Q144: d: David Copeland Over three successive weekends, Copeland placed homemade nail bombs (each containing up to 1,500 four-inch nails) outside a supermarket in Electric Avenue, Brixton, an area of south London with a large black population; in Brick Lane in the east end of London, which has a large South Asian community; and in the Admiral Duncan pub in Soho's Old Compton Street, the heart of London's gay community The bombs killed three (including a pregnant woman), and injured 129 (four of whom lost limbs). No warnings were given.

Q145: c: Ian Kay. Kay was sentenced, in 1995, for a minimum term of 22 years imprisonment for the murder of 21-year-old John Penfold, a Woolworth's shop assistant stabbed to death in Teddington, Middlesex, in November 1994. Kay was on leave from prison, almost eight years after nearly killing another shop worker in a similar attack, when he killed Penfold, whom he described as a "Have-a-go-hero who got what he deserved". Kay was transferred to Broadmoor after showing signs of mental illness. On March 10 1997, while in Broadmoor, Kay attempted to kill Peter Sutcliffe, stabbing him six times in the left eye and four times in the right eye with a Parker Rollerball pen (used during the hospital's drawing classes), blinding Sutcliffe in the left eye and severely damaging his right eye. On trial on January 28 1998, Kay admitted stabbing Sutcliffe, and told the court that he had intended to attack him with a razor embedded in a toothbrush handle. Kay said, "I was going to walk into the room and cut his jugular vein on both sides and wait there until he was dead. Killing has always been in my mind, ever since I've been here [at Broadmoor]. In hindsight, I should have straddled him and strangled him with my bare hands. He said God told him to kill thirteen women, and I say the devil told me to kill him because of that".

Q146: c: Roy Shaw. The name Roy 'Pretty Boy' Shaw was used as his fight name in his unlicensed boxing tournaments; an excellent natural boxer, Roy was too old to fight professionally when he was released from prison, so unlicensed boxing was the only option for him. He quickly built up a fearsome reputation for himself which still stands today.

Q147: d: Dave Courtney. Dave came up into the public eye after organising the security at Ronnie Kray's funeral. His contacts within the underworld were so vast that he was the source everyone went to when they needed to contact someone in that secret circle. He is well-known for his celebrity shows in which he talks about his life. His favourite phrase is: 'I'm not hard, but I have a phonebook full of hard bastards".

Q148: b: Howard Marks. In the mid-eighties, Howard had forty-three aliases, eighty-nine phone lines and twenty-five companies trading all over the world; and he was smuggling up to thirty-two tonnes (per consignment) of hashish from Pakistan and Thailand to the US and Canada. He has since published three hugely successful books, the first of which - 'Mr Nice' - got its name from his favourite alias: 'Donald Nice'.

Q149: d: Wandsworth, Belmarsh and Wormwood Scrubs. Jim served in these prisons between 1992 and 1999.

Q150: a: Gary Taylor. Gary Taylor is a former strongman and prison service physical training instructor from Wales, who won the World's Strongest Man contest in 1993. His strongman career ended in 1997 when he sustained a serious leg injury in the tire flip contest in Holland. A former weightlifter, powerlifter and bodybuilder, Taylor competed in weightlifting at the 1984 Summer Olympics in Los Angeles, taking second in the snatch.

Q151: a: Frank Mitchell. Frank Mitchell was a giant of a man, with a long history of violent behaviour (due, largely, to his having severe learning disabilities). He got the nickname 'the Mad Axeman' after breaking out of Broadmoor special hospital, breaking into a cottage to take refuge, and sitting in the front room there, guarding the couple whose home it was with a large axe on his lap.

Q152: c: Dartmoor

Q153: c: Broadmoor

Q154: c: Frankie Fraser

Q155: a: Parkhurst, Hull, Leicester, Winchester, Wandsworth and Broadmoor

Q156: b: Shepton Mallet

Q157: b: October 24 1933. Reggie was born at 8:00am, and his identical twin brother, Ronnie, was born at 8:10am.

Q158: c: March 17 1995. At the age of 61, Ronnie Kray died of a heart attack in Wexham Park Hospital in Slough, Berkshire. His death was due to his smoking 100 cigarettes a day. He was buried at Chingford Cemetery, near the bodies of his father, mother, and sister.

Q159: a: October 1 2000. On August 16 2000, Reggie was released from prison on compassionate grounds, as he was dying of bladder cancer. The same day, with his wife at his bedside, Reggie passed away.

Q160: a: The Blind Beggar. On March 9 1966, Ronnie shot and killed George Cornell at the Blind Beggar. Cornell was killed to avenge the death of one of their gang members, Richard Hart.

Q161: d: 1969

Q162: d: Leonard 'Nipper' Reed

Q163: a: Mickey McAvoy. 'The Brinks Mat Robbery' occurred on November 26 1983, when six robbers broke into the Brinks Mat warehouse at Heathrow Airport, England. The robbers thought they were going to steal £3 million in cash; but, when they arrived, they found ten tonnes of gold bullion (worth £26 million). The gang got into the warehouse with help from security guard Anthony Black, the brother-in-law of Brian Robinson (who came up with the idea for the raid). Scotland Yard quickly discovered the family connection and Black confessed to aiding and abetting the raiders: providing them with a key to the main door and giving them details of security measures.

Q164: c: 25. Tried at the Old Bailey, Robinson and gang leader Michael McAvoy were each sentenced to 25 years imprisonment for armed robbery. Three tonnes of the stolen gold has never been recovered, and it has been claimed that anyone wearing gold jewellery bought in the UK after 1983 is probably wearing proceeds from the Brinks Mat Robbery.

Q165: a: Michael Peterson. Bronson states on his website that (contrary to reports frequently made in the press), his name was changed by his fight promoter in 1987, and was not a choice he made in relation to the actor, Charles Bronson.

Q166: c: 1974, armed robbery. Charles Bronson has been in prison since the age of nineteen for various offences. Initially jailed in 1974 for robbery, his sentence has been repeatedly extended and he has spent only three months out of custody.

Q167: b: 2000. In 2000, he received a discretionary life sentence (with a three year tariff) for a hostage-taking incident. His appeal against this sentence was denied in 2004.

Q168: a: Taking a civilian teacher hostage. In 2000, Charlie received a discretionary life sentence (with a three year tariff) for taking civilian teacher, Phil Danielson, hostage. Despite numerous media reports and popular belief, Charlie has never killed anyone. His appeal against this sentence was denied in 2004; however, he has a huge network of supporters and a legal team fighting for his release.

Q169: c: 120+ Bronson has been in prison since the age of nineteen. Initially jailed in 1974 for robbery, his sentence has been repeatedly extended for offences against prison discipline (in reaction to often harsh treatment by staff). He has spent only three months out of custody. He has served over thirty years of his time in prison in solitary confinement, and has spent time in over 120 different prisons. His story is told in greater detail in his ten published books, as well as in 'The Loose Screw' by Jim Dawkins (an ex-Prison-Officer who spent months looking after Charlie in prison and is still a good friend and supporter of his today).

Q170: a: Harry Roberts. Harry Maurice Roberts was a career criminal with convictions for attempted store-breaking, larceny and robbery with violence. He was a former soldier who had served in Malaya. He almost certainly opened fire because he thought that the policemen were about to search the van and believed he would get fifteen years if he was caught with a firearm. Roberts is one of the UK's most notorious murderers and longest-serving prison inmates. He is known, in the Prison Service, as 'Hate em all Harry'.

RECENT PRISON FACTS

Q171: d: The five main types of prison in Britain today are:
1: Local prisons (that takes those who are still awaiting trial or sentencing, and other short sentence prisoners)
2: Young offenders institutions (for 15-20-year-olds, inclusive)
3: Women's prisons
4: Training prisons (some of which are open and hold long sentence prisoners approaching release)
5: High security prisons (housing the country's most dangerous criminals, many of which are serving life sentences; these prisons are often referred to as 'Dispersal Prisons')

Q172: b: 1936. The first open prison in Britain held fifty men. More open prisons opened after the Second World War, cheaply constructed out of disused armed forces camps. The open prison was set up initially as a way of relieving pressure in overcrowded closed prisons.

Q173: a: New Hall Camp. Open prisons were started as an emergency measure to ease overcrowding; and, as a result, were hastily opened, without adequate rules in place to guide them. Most were run, consequently, like closed prisons without the perimeter walls. Many say that doing time in an open prison is psychologically harder to deal with, because prisoners face a 'mental' barrier rather than a stone one.

Q174: a: Wakefield. The first open prison was an annexe of Wakefield

Prison and held fifty men in dormitory huts. The men held here worked either on local farms or making boots.

Q175: c: England and Wales

Q176: a: 11. Privately-managed prisons were introduced in the UK in the 1990s. HM Chief Inspectorate of Prisons inspects private prisons in the same way as it inspects public sector prisons. (See 'How Prisons are Regulated' for more information.) All private prisons have a 'Controller' linking them to the Home Office, and the governors of private prisons are called 'Directors'.

Q177: c: 128

Q178: d: 85%

Q179: b: Slade Prison was the fictional prison setting for that hugely successful and highly accurate comic portrayal of prison life Porridge.

Q180: True. Latchmere was used by MI5 from 1939. They held captured German spies here, and attempted to turn them into double agents. Those who refused were hanged as enemy spies.

Q181: c: 1969

Q182: d: Stanford University. The Stanford experiment ended on August 20 1971 - only 6 days after it began, and 8 days early. The experiment very quickly got out of hand. Prisoners suffered sadistic and humiliating treatment at the hands of the guards; and, by the end, many showed severe emotional disturbance. As the experiment proceeded, several of the guards became progressively more sadistic. The experiment's observers said that approximately one-third of the guards exhibited 'genuine' sadistic tendencies, and, interestingly, most of the guards were upset when the experiment was cut off early.

Q183: True. The borstal system was constantly under scrutiny amid allegations of staff brutality and being a breeding ground for bullies and psychopaths. The system was finally replaced in 1982 with Youth Custody Centres.

Q184: c: Prison Officers Association. This is the Prison Service's trade union - at one time, the largest trade union in the country.

Q185: a: 3 - Parkhurst, Albany and Camp Hill

Q186: c: Kingston

Q187: a: Brixton, Pentonville, Wandsworth, Wormwood Scrubs, Belmarsh and Holloway

Q188: d: HMP Albany on the Isle of Wight

Q189: a: Belmarsh

Q190: b: Strangeways. After the Strangeways riot, the government introduced a new charge of 'prison mutiny' (which carried a ten-year sentence) and with which the ringleaders of the riots were charged.

Q191: Category A, B, C, and D. Category A is the highest category, and D the lowest.

Q192: a: £37,500

Q193: d: Wandsworth Prison is the largest prison in London, and the second largest in the country.

Q194: c: Liverpool

Q195: a: Central Prison

Q196: a: Brixton Prison Hospital. Until Belmarsh Healthcare Centre opened in the early 90s, Brixton's hospital wing held some of the worse cases of mentally ill prisoners in the system.

Q197: a: 3. All were recaptured fairly quickly and the escape forced the resignation of the Prison's Governor.

Q198: c: 1990s

Q199: c: 1932

Q200: a: The Duchy of Cornwall

Q201: b: 1990. The riots lasted from April 1 to April 25 1990, and the scenes of hooded prisoners on the roof with their hostages were rarely off the television screens.

Q202: b: Parkhurst was originally a Military Barracks

Q203: c: Alcatraz

Q204: a: A prison cell. A 'kishka' is a type of prison cell used in Soviet prisons. The cell was named after the gut (kishka), because they were tall and narrow - apparently like an intestine, but probably more like a chimney. The prisoner had room to stand, but could not sit or kneel - let alone lie down. In some Soviet prisons, there was no drainage and the prisoner was forced to excrete standing up, and then stand in his own urine and faeces. In some cases, the cells were never cleaned. Prisoners could be held in these cells for months at a time.

Q205: c: The Clink

Q206:+ a: Sing Sing. This 'correctional facility' is a maximum security prison in Ossining, New York, USA. Sing Sing's history – reaches back almost to the beginning of the state prison system in New York. The name comes from the original name of the town of Ossining, although the penitentiary was called 'Mount Pleasant' when it opened in 1828. In 1825, the state legislature gave the job of building a modern prison to Captain Elam Lynds, a prison warden from upstate New York.

Q207: a: Category A Prisoners are those whose escape would be highly dangerous to the public or national security.

Q208: c: Category B prisoners are those who don't require maximum security, but for whom escape needs to be made very difficult.

Q209: b: Category C prisoners are those who can't be trusted in open conditions, but who are unlikely to try to escape.

Q210: d: Category D prisoners are trusted enough to wander freely within the prison, but must show up for several daily roll-calls.

Q211: b: Someone who reports on prison conditions, but is independent of the Prison Service.

Q212: c: New entrant Prison Officer. All new Prison Officers normally spend two weeks in a jail local to their home, where they wear a suit and carry only a whistle on a chain, a notebook and a prison cap badge on their lapels as identification. This is a nerve-wracking time, as many older staff and prisoners take every opportunity to intimidate new staff. It is during this time that they are called NEPOs.

Q213: a: Health Care Officer. Most prison hospitals are staffed mainly by civillian psychiatric nurses; although there are Prison Health Care Officers who are fully qualified nurses and have completed the full Prison Service Officer training course. These officers wear Prison Officer uniforms with a 'H' on their epaulettes.

Q214: c: 5. There are currently five grades of Governor: Governor five being the most junior and Governor one being the highest ranking. There is usually only one Governor to each prison, and s/he is in overall charge of that particular establishment.

Q215: a: Prison officer, senior officer, principle officer. These are the three uniformed grades of Regular Landing Prison Officers; in addition, there are auxiliary officers who carry out important tasks such as gate duties, running prison canteens and driving prison vans.

Q216: True. The Chief Officer was like an Army RSM in all aspects, and was the God-like presence responsible for the discipline of staff and inmates alike. Many older members of staff (and indeed old lags) blame the removal of the Chief Officers for today's apparent lack of discipline and the prevalence of bullying in many prisons.

Q217: c: 1992. The Prison Service stopped teaching its new recruits drill in 1992. The last course to be taught drill - and therefore, put on a passing out parade - was course NR22 at Prison Service College, Newbold Revel, in September 1992.

Q218: a: Belmarsh. Shortly after the prison became operational in April 1991, a prisoner on a visit managed to swap places with one of his male visitors and walk out of the prison unchallenged. Prisoners in Belmarsh wore their own clothes, and - when on visits - the only way to distinguish a prisoner from a visitor was by the netball-style sports vest prisoners wore over their clothes. All the prisoner had to do was give this vest to his visitor and walk out in his place!

Q219: d: Organising and supervising the wing's general daily administration. The Wing Cleaning Officer's job is often a thankless task that involves duties such as the collection and distribution of meals, stores, clothing and bedding, as well as supervising landing cleaners and canteen runs, etc.

Q220: a: When a prisoner too far from home for his family to visit saves up his visits entitlement.

Q221: False. A prisoner can request a temporary transfer for accumulated visits to a local prison, but he cannot pay for transport himself. However, these transfers must not cost the Prison Service any money, so they are arranged to coincide with pre-planned prison transfers (arranged for court appearances and other legal reasons), and the prisoner on temporary transfer is moved in the same transport.

Q222: c: A lie down

Q223: d: A chain with three individual handcuffs attached for use during prison escorts

Q224: d: To allow a prisoner to go to the toilet during an escort, whilst remaining securely attached to the escorting officer outside the door.

Q225: a: Inside Times

Q226: b: 1990

Q227: d: 2007

CELEBRITY PRISONERS

Q228: b: The Man in Black. By the early 1970s, Cash had crystallised his public image as 'The Man in Black'. He regularly performed dressed all in black, wearing a long, black, knee-length coat. This outfit stood in stark contrast to the costumes worn by most of the major country acts in his day: rhinestone suit and cowboy boots. Cash felt great compassion for prisoners and, in the late 50s, began performing concerts at various prisons. These performances led to a pair of highly successful live albums: 'Johnny Cash at Folsom Prison' (1968) and 'Johnny Cash at San Quentin' (1969).

Q229: c: Lester Piggott. Lester Keith Piggott is a retired English jockey, considered to be the best of his generation and one of the greatest flat jockeys of all time. He achieved 4,493 career wins, including 9 Derby victories. In 1987, he was jailed for 3 years for tax irregularities, of which he served 366 days. The following year he was stripped of the OBE he had been awarded in 1975. He resumed his career as a jockey in 1990, winning the Breeders' Cup Mile on Royal Academy within 10 days of his return, and riding another classic winner, Rodrigo de Triano, in 1992. He rode his last winner in October 1994, and officially retired in 1995.

Q230: b: Terry Marsh. Terry Marsh was born on February 7 1958, in Stepney, East London, but later moved to Basildon, Essex., He was a highly talented amateur and professional boxer. His career was cut short when he was forced to retire (due to illness) at the age of 29, only 4 months after winning a world title. Consequently, he is the only English boxer ever to retire as an undefeated World Champion. At this point, his life changed in a number of ways: In 1989, his manager, Frank Warren, was shot and Marsh was tried for his attempted murder. He was subsequently acquitted.

Q231: a: John Bindon. Bindon was a British actor and bodyguard, noted for his film roles as a London underworld figure and tough police detective. He was also running a protection racket in west London, targeting pubs, restaurants and cafes. In 1978, Bindon became involved in a fight with John Darke, at the Ranelagh Yacht Club, in Fulham, London. Darke was stabbed 9 times, and Bindon managed to flee to Dublin with his own knife wounds covered up. He later gave himself up to police and, in his trial at the Old Bailey in November 1979, was acquitted of Darke's murder - thanks, mainly, to Bob Hoskins, who testified as a character witness. During the 1980s, Bindon became a virtual recluse and heroin addict. He died in London at the Chelsea and Westminster Hospital on October 10 1993 from complications as a result of AIDS.

Q232: b: Mark 'the Mac' Morrison. He spent a number of months on B wing at Wormwood Scrubs, where he was subjected by many Prison Officers to a fairly tough time, due to his celebrity status.

Q233: b: Sammy McCarthy

Q234: c: Jeffrey Archer. Lord Archer has written a series of books based on his experiences inside. They are titled, 'Prison Diaries' and are a great read!

Q235: a: Jonathan Aitkin. He was jailed for perjury and perverting the course of justice.

Q236: a: Lord Brocket

Q237: b: Roy James

Q238: c: George Best. George Best was a Northern Irish football player, best known for his years with Manchester United. In 1984, Best received a three-month prison sentence for drunk driving, assaulting a police officer and failing to bail. He spent Christmas of 1984 behind bars and turned out as a player for Ford Open Prison.

Q239: a: Lord Brocket. He was convicted for conspiracy to commit car insurance fraud after he dismantled four Ferraris and hid them, claiming to police that they had been stolen.

Q240: d: Lord Brocket was stabbed by a fellow inmate and consequently moved to Ford Open Prison.

Q241: b: Lord Brocket plays the part of a policeman in Dave Courtney's upcoming DVD film about the club scene, 'Clubbing To Death'.

PRISON-RELATED FILM AND TELEVISION

Q242: c: Number Six

Q243: b: Burt Reynolds. The film was remade in the late and starred ex-footballer and Hollywood actor, Vinnie Jones, alongside Jason Statham; and was set in a fictional British prison.

Q244: d: 1979. Scum is 1979 film, portraying the brutality of life inside a British borstal. It tells the story of Carlin, a young offender, who arrives at the institution and rises to the top of the inmates' pecking order by using violence to survive. The film is an indictment of the borstal system: its ineffectiveness at rehabilitating inmates and likelihood of contributing to the youths becoming even more broken individuals.

Q245: b: Vinnie Jones

Q246: d: Martin and Gary Kemp from Spandau Ballet.

Q247: a: The Goss Brothers

Q248: b: Jason Statham. Statham was born in Sydenham, Lewisham, London, the second son of a lounge singer and dressmaker-turned-dancer who ran a black market operation. Statham's life in media began when he was spotted by a talent agent specialising in athletes, while training at London's Crystal Palace National Sports Centre. Afterwards, he became a model for the clothing brand, French Connection, where he was introduced to then-fledgling British director,

Guy Ritchie. Ritchie was working on a film project and needed to fill the role of a streetwise con artist. After learning about Statham's past, Ritchie cast him to play the role of 'Bacon' in Ritchie's breakout 1998 hit, 'Lock, Stock and Two Smoking Barrels'. The movie was well received by both critics and audiences, which catapulted the unknown actor into the public eye. Statham's second collaboration with Ritchie came in the 2000 film, 'Snatch'. Cast alongside Brad Pitt, Dennis Farina and Benicio Del Toro - and with the movie earning more than $80 million in box-office revenues, Statham was able to break into Hollywood, and appeared in two movies in 2001: John Carpenter's 'Ghosts of Mars' and the Jet Li vehicle, 'The One'.

Q249: Mr McKay and Mr Barraclough

Q250: The actor was the late, great Ronnie Barker, and his character was 'Norman Stanley Fletcher'.

Q251: c: David Jason (Del Boy in 'Only Fools And Horses'). Jason also played alongside the late great Ronnie Barker in Open All Hours as G-G-G-Granville, the bungling bakery delivery boy.

Q252: c: Dave Courtney

Q253: b: Barbara Windsor was married to Ronnie Knight, visiting him in prison many times.

Q254: a: Prisoner Cell Block H

Q255: b: Bad Girls

Q256: c: Slade

Q257: d: David Dickinson

Q258: c: Leslie Grantham. Leslie was convicted in 1966 of the murder of a German taxi driver whilst he was a young soldier serving in Osnabruck.

Q259: c: Two Way Stretch

Q260: a: Freddie Foreman

Q261: c: Bob Hoskins

Q262: c: Tom Hardy

Q263: d: Get Carter

Q264: b: The Italian Job. This film was a great attack on the prison authorities as it showed the whole job being planned from inside the prison, by the 'Daddy'.

PRISON PUNISHMENTS

Q265: c: A form of medieval stocks, where a petty criminal is locked by the head and hands for public humiliation. The pillory consisted of hinged wooden boards with holes for the head and/or limbs. The boards were locked together to secure the captive. Pillories were set up in marketplaces and crossroads to hold petty criminals, and often a placard detailing the crime was placed nearby. These punishments generally lasted only a few hours. Time in the pillory was more dangerous than in the stocks, as the pillory forced the malfeasant to remain standing and exposed.

Q266: a: The Treadwheel. Cubitt devised the Treadwheel in 1817 after being approached by an Ipswich Magistrate looking to suppress civil disorder in East Anglia.

Q267: a: Brixton. The Treadwheel was one of a number of non-productive activities introduced in our early prisons. The resistance of the wheel could be increased by warders tightening the tension screws, thus making the wheel harder for prisoners to rotate.

Q268: d: 48-50 steps per minute. The Treadwheel was soon classed by most as an instrument of torture, but was enthusiastically embraced by others who enjoyed watching the spectacle. One magistrate even stated it was "The most tiresome, distressing, exemplary punishment that has ever been contrived by human ingenuity".

Q269: a: York Castle Prison. The wheel was dismantled after their use was suspended on April 1 1902, classified as an excessive form of hard labour. This last wheel is now on display at Madame Tussauds.

Q270: c: 1968

Q271: b: 6 stitches to every inch

Q272: a: Yellow and green striped

Q273: b: Good Order and Discipline. This charge covers many offences, and is the most common one used by prison staff to place an inmate on report.

Q274: c: 1922

Q275: c: Fourteen days cellular confinement. This is a punishment in which the prisoner is stripped of everything in his cell, apart from a chair, a table, a book and a bible, from morning to dusk.

Q276: b: An adjudication hearing

Q277: a: Rule 45 is the segregation of vulnerable prisoners. Prisoners on Rule 45 are usually those convicted of crimes of a sexual nature or those who - for various reasons - cannot survive on a normal prison wing. A prisoner convicted of sexual crimes will be offered Rule 45 on arrival in prison, but they are not obliged to accept it, and can choose to take their chances on the normal wings. Non-vulnerable prisoners can be segregated under Rule 45 GOAD, which is a separate prison rule usually awarded on adjudication.

Q278: c: 1962

Q279: d: 28. A prisoner can be held in segregation (not to be confused with cellular confinement) for a maximum period of 28 days, after which their position must be reviewed - and, in certain circumstances - a further award given.

Q280: a: Wandsworth. Wandsworth was chosen to hold stocks of the 'judicial birch', and here they were to be "thoroughly tested" before being supplied to a prison when a prisoner was sentenced to be birched.

Q281: b: Eric Mason

Q282: a: 'The Liquid Cosh'. This was very often named 'cold steel' by prisoners/patients who have suffered a dose of this muscle-wasting drug.

Q283: d: F1145

Q284: a: Loss of privileges, stoppage of earnings, cellular confinement, added days and exclusion from work.

Q285: c: 42

Q286: c: 21

Q287: a: 21

Q288: c: 25. Offences against discipline numbers 1, 17, 20 and 24 also have a part two that is slightly reworded to include racially-motivated offences.

Q289: a: Rule 51. Rule 51 sets out the offences against prison discipline for which a prisoner can be charged. Young offenders institutions are covered by the Young Offenders Rule 55, which is very similar.

Q290: True. Prison Rule 22 and Young Offenders Rule 25 state, "It is an offence to disobey any lawful order", and Prison Rule 23 and Young Offenders Rule 26 state, "It is an offence fail to comply with any rule or regulation of the prison".

PRISON SLANG

Q291: Bang up

Q292: 'The Baron' is the person on the wing or landing who controls the smuggling and distribution of illicit articles with bullying or his position in the pecking order. These items could be tobacco, drugs, etc.; hence, 'The Drug Baron' and 'The Tobacco Baron'.

Q293: 'Bird' or 'Bit', e.g. "Just doing my bird" or "I got a six year bit".

Q294: 'Criminal Charges' (e.g. "I got a robbery beef this time") or 'a problem' (e.g. "I've got a real beef with that guy").

Q295: A 'cell soldier' is someone who gives it the big one when the cells are locked: dishing out threats or bragging about his escapades out the cell window, but who typically becomes as quiet as a mouse when his cell door is open.

Q296: A 'kanga' is a prison officer. It is an abbreviation of Kangaroo: cockney rhyming slang for 'screw', a common name for Prison Officers.

Q297: A 'peter' is a cell. The word is believed to have come from 'rabbit hutch' (i.e. Peter Rabbit), comparing the size of a prison cell with that of a rabbit hutch.

Q298: c: "I got a knock back."

Q299: He would be up in front of the Parole Board (again, 'Jam Roll' being cockney rhyming slang - this time for parole).

Q300: In the segregation unit

Q301: A 'Durham nip' is the name given to a particularly skinny self-rolled cigarette, popular in prisons due to limited access to the canteen.

Q302: A cigarette. A 'tailor-made' is a proper, factory-made cigarette that you would buy in a pack from the newsagents.

Q303: A nonce is a 'sex case', or someone convicted for crimes of a sexual nature. It can also be used to describe any one choosing to be located on the 'vulnerable prisoner wing'. They are also referred to as 'beasts'.

Q304: A 'grass' is the name given to a prison informant. The name is derived from the 70s song 'Whispering Grass', sung by Windsor Davies and Don Estelle. The song was number one in the charts for three weeks from June 1 1975, and coincided with the emergence of the 'supergrass' informers.

Q305: a: A sweat box

Q306: b: Coming off drugs. The phrase comes from the better known saying 'cold turkey', i.e. 'clucking like a turkey'.

Q307: c: The spy hole on a cell door. This is how staff make their checks on prisoners during lock-up periods and at night; and prisoners are often caught breaking rules by staff creeping up to quietly observe them: hence the name 'Judas hole'.

Q308: b: Dedicated staff cell-searching teams

Q309: c: The specially-trained riot squads. In the early days - before the introduction of 'Control and Restraint Level 2 Riot Training', these 'Mufti Squads' were typically made up of the biggest officers, armed with two-foot long, wooden batons and prison issue mattresses as makeshift shields.

Q310: c: A potent alcoholic brew made in secret by prisoners

Q311: d: Human waste wrapped in paper and thrown out of a cell window at night. This practice was more common in jails that did not have integral sanitation in the cells, and served two objectives: to prevent the smell of human waste engulfing the cell all night and to annnoy the outside dog patrols who regularly made sweeps of the sterile area between the cell walls and prison perimeter.

Q312: a: When a prisoner is moved from one prison to another, in quick succession and without prior knowledge, for reasons of ensuring good order and discipline.

SEX OFFENDERS

Q313: b: Ashworth Special Hospital

Q314: c: John Straffen

Q315: d: 13

Q316: b: The Yorkshire Ripper case. Wearside Jack was the nickname given to John Samuel Humble (born January 8 1956), a hoaxer who pretended to be the Yorkshire Ripper in the late 1970s. On March 21 2006, Humble was sentenced to eight years in jail.

Q317: Bronzefield

Q318: d: 37

Q319: a: West Suffolk Hospital

Q320: True

Q321: d: No one knows. There were suspicious deaths when Shipman was in Todmorden, but the time at which the killing started has never been confirmed. Most of the bodies were too badly decomposed to be tested for the presence of morphine, and therefore cannot be officially classed as victims.

Q322: False. Dr Shipman has failed to admit to his crimes or show any remorse.

Q323: c: The Drowning Man. "The Drowning Man" has never been published, as authorities at Whitemoor top security prison (where Nilsen was first imprisoned) confiscated the manuscript in 2001, along with an anthology of poems Nilsen had written. Nilsen appealed to the High Court to have the manuscript returned to him, but this was rejected. Nilsen has also applied for permission to have pornography.

Q324: Ivan Lawrence QC. Nilsen went on trial for the murders of six men, and the attempted murder of two others, on October 24 1983 London's Old Bailey. Ivan Lawrence, one of Britain's finest legal minds, argued that Nilsen wa suffering from a mental illness at the time of his crimes. Nilsen was found guilty of all the murders and sentenced to life imprisonment with a recommendation that he serve a minimum of 25 years.

Q325: d: A plumber called to inspect a blockage and found rotting flesh in his drains. In February 1983, other tenants in Nilsen's block of flats complained of toilets not flushing properly and called in a specialist drain clearance company. Engineer, Mike Cattran, inspected a drainage pit and found it full of - what looked and smelled like - rotting flesh. When he brought his boss back to take a look the next day, the flesh had mysteriously gone, but there were skin and bone fragments left in the pipes and the concerned plumber phoned the police.

Q326: Gary Glitter

Q327: Glitter was charged with committing obscene acts with minors, for which he was found guilty and received a three-year prison sentence.

Q328: a: Roy Whiting. On December 12 2001, Roy Whiting was convicted of the abduction and murder of Sarah Payne and sentenced to life imprisonment. The trial judge, Mr Justice Curtis, said that it was a rare case in which a life sentence should mean life. This was only the 24th time in British legal history that such a recommendation had been made.,After Whiting was convicted of killing Sarah Payne, it was revealed that he was already a convicted child sex offender, proving correct the Payne family's belief that this was the case. There were renewed calls for the government to allow controlled public access to the sex offender's register. (This became the campaign for 'Sarah's Law', after 'Megan's Law' in America.)

Q329: c: Wakefield. On August 4 2002, Whiting was attacked in

Wakefield Prison by a prisoner with a razor, while fetching hot water. Convicted killer, Rickie Tregaskis, was found guilty of carrying out the slashing that left Whiting with a six-inch scar on his right cheek. Tregaskis, serving life for the murder of a disabled man in Cornwall, received a six-year sentence (to run concurrently alongside his life sentence) in June 2004.

HIGH-RISK LIFE-SENTENCED PRISONERS

Q330: a: An 'automatic lifer' is a person aged 18 or over, sentenced to life for a second, serious, sexual or violent offence committed on or after October 1 1997.

Q331: c: A 'discretionary life sentence' is a life sentence given by the courts for a serious offence (other than murder), which is not a 'mandatory' sentence.

Q332: a: Discretionary Lifer Panel. This is the panel of the parole board that carries out hearings for discretionary life prisoners.

Q333: d: A 'mandatory life sentence' is the sentence a court must give for a conviction of murder.

Q334: b: The Lifer Unit is the part of Prison Service Headquarters, at Abel house, London, that deals with the management and reviews of all lifer cases.

Q335: a: A tariff is the part of a prisoner's life sentence that must be served in prison, both as a punishment for them and a deterrent to others. It is extremely rare that a prisoner is released before their tariff date.

Q336: c: Frankland, Full Sutton, Long Lartin and Wakefield Whitemoor

Q337: c: Belmarsh, Whitemoor and Wakefield

Q338: a: Wakefield. HMP Wakefield is located in Wakefield, West Yorkshire, England. It was originally built as a house of correction, in 1594, and is now the largest maximum security prison in the United Kingdom. The current building was built in Victorian times.

Q339: b: Life Sentence Plan. Every life-sentenced prisoner has his or her own LSP. It contains details of their offending behaviour that needs to be addressed, and is reviewed annually by staff using reports of the prisoner's behaviour throughout the year. The prisoner should get the opportunity to see his plan and comment on its findings.

Q340: a: An 'escorted absence' is where category C lifers, subject to certain conditions, undertake familiarisation visits to a local town, under supervision by a Prison Officer.

Q341: c: A 'First Stage Prison' is a prison that specialises in assessing newly-convicted lifers and prepares their Life Sentence Plans.
Q342: a: A 'Second Stage Prison' is a prison that specialises in accommodating lifers for the main part of their sentences. These are usually category B or C prisons.

Q343: c: Whitemoor. In September 1994, six prisoners (including five IRA members) escaped from the prison's Special Secure Unit after smuggling guns into the prison. All were later recaptured.

BASIC PRISON RULES AND REGULATIONS

Q344: b: 3. The three people limit counts for all visitors who are aged ten years and over.

Q345: a: Every working day, i.e. Monday to Friday (or at least three of these days, during the period in which visiting hours are normally held). They are entitled to at least fifteen minutes per visit; and in addition, prisoners can, each fortnight, also receive a visit on a Saturday or Sunday.

Q346: c: Christmas Day, Boxing Day and Good Friday

Q347: b: 2. A convicted prisoner is entitled to a minimum of two visits every four weeks, which should be for a duration of 60 minutes each.

Q348: d: Up to 42

Q349: a: 3 months

Q350: b: 2

Q351: a: 1

Q352: d: The rule that ensures legal documents are posted in to inmates without being opened and or read. All letters covered by Rule 39 should be marked clearly with 'Rule 39' on the envelope. These letters can be sealed before you hand them in for posting, unlike personal letters, which must be left unsealed.

Q353: False. Due to the need to censor all category A prisoners' mail, prisoners in this category may not write letters in any language. All other category prisoners are permitted to do so.

Q354: c: Counselling, advice, referral, assessment and thorough care. Every prison now has 'CARAT' workers, whose job it is to make sure that prisoners with drug problems get help and advice on how to tackle their addictions.

Q355: b: 25

Q356: a: F1127. This form should be given to a prisoner at least two hours before any adjudication hearing, and has a space on the back for the prisoner to prepare a defence statement.

Q357: c: Actual release date. If sentenced to up to twelve months, a prisoner's 'actual release date' is the date s/he should be released.

Q358: b: Half. A prisoner serving twelve months or less will be eligible for release at the halfway point of their sentence on 'good behaviour'.

Q359: a: Sentence expiry date. A prisoners SED is the date his/her complete sentence expires; in other words, it is the full length of the sentence given.

Q360: c: The next working day after sentencing

Q361: d: Home detention curfew. This is where a prisoner serving four years or less may be released before their actual release date but be subject to a curfew. This means that they have to be at a designated address at certain times arranged prior to release. These days, prisoners released under this scheme are usually fitted with an electronic tag.

Q362: a: Conditional release date. The conditional release date applies to prisoners sentenced to between twelve months and four years. It is the halfway point of their sentence, and they will have the conditions set out for release at this point.

Q363: c: **Three-quarter point.** If a prisoner is serving between twelve months and four years, they should be released under supervision halfway through the sentence. The supervision conditions (e.g. reporting to a Probation Officer) are usually in force up until the three-quarter point of the original sentence.

Q364: a: **Parole eligibility date.** This applies to all prisoners serving sentences of four years or more, and is the earliest date at which they are eligible for release (formerly known as the EDR: earliest date of release).

Q365: b: **Additional days awarded.** These are days added to a prisoner's sentence as punishment for breaking prison rules during their incarceration.

Q366: a: **Basic, standard and enhanced**

Q367: c: **Private cash**

Q368: a: **£250**

Q369: c: **£1000**

Q370: b: **£1500**

Q371: d: **£15 for prisoners on the lowest regime and £30 for prisoners on the middle or top regimes.**

Q372: a: **The conviction is unsafe or unsatisfactory, there was a wrong decision on a question of law or there was a material irregularity in the course of the trial.** The Court of Appeal has wide powers for calling witnesses and evidence, including witnesses who were called at the original trial.

Many other countries provide an automatic right of appeal, which addresses the possibility that a jury may have come to a mistaken verdict. There is no such right in England and Wales.

Q373: b: **Every 15 minutes.** For each prisoner on 'suicide watch', staff must fill out an observation book every fifteen minutes to confirm s/he has physically checked the prisoner and had a positive response from them.

SCOTLAND AND IRELAND

Q374: a: **Robert Leslie Stewart.** Stewart was from Edinburgh, Scotland,

and one of the last executioners in the United Kingdom, officiating between 1950 and 1964.

Q375: c: Swansea Prison. Stewart carried out the last execution in Wales. In May 1958, Vivian Teed was executed at Swansea Prison for the murder of a postmaster during a robbery.

Q376: a: Crumlin Road Prison. Harry Allen performed the last execution in Northern Ireland when he hanged Robert McGladdery in Crumlin Road Prison, Belfast, in December 1961.

Q377: c: Peter Moore. Peter Moore is a Welsh serial killer who murdered four men in Wales in 1995. Between September and December that year, he stabbed four randomly-selected men to death, and was also responsible for torturing more than fifty men. When Moore was arrested, he claimed his next intended victim was his bank manager and that he had an alter-ego, named Jason, who had committed the crimes. He was sentenced to life imprisonment in 1996.

Q378: b: Aberdeen Prison. Harry Allen performed the last hanging in Scotland when he hanged Henry Burnett in Aberdeen on August 15 1963 for the murder of Thomas Guyan.

Q379: c: 15. This figure includes two young offender prisons at Falkirk and Stirling, three open prisons at Perth, Kinross and Angus and one women's prison at Stirling. There is also one privately-run prison, Kilmarnock, which is controlled by SERCO.

Q380: b: Glasgow. HMP Barlinnie is located in the residential suburb of Riddrie, north-east of Glasgow, Scotland. It was mainly used for short-term prisoners and those awaiting trial in Glasgow courts, but also long-term prisoners awaiting transfer to prisons such as Saughton or Peterhead. Barlinnie Prison consists of five halls: A, B, C, D and E; and is colloquially known as 'Bar-L'. The bucket-as-toilet routine (known as 'slopping out') was still in practice there as late as 2003. Since 2001, refurbishment has taken place after critical reports by the Scottish Chief Inspector of Prisons.

Q381: a: 7. Peter Manuel (March 1 1927 – July 11 1958) was a US-born, British serial killer who committed his crimes in Scotland. At his trial at Glasgow High Court, Manuel conducted his own defence but was unable to convince the judge of his insanity plea. He was found guilty in May 1958 of seven murders, although many connected with the case believe he killed closer to 15 people.

Q382: b: Barlinnie. Manuel was hanged at Barlinnie Prison in Glasgow on July 11 1958. He was the second-to-last person to be hanged in Barlinnie Prison, and the third-to-last to be hanged in Scotland. Scottish actor, Brian Cox, is said to have based his portrayal of 'Hannibal Lecter' in 'Manhunter' on Manuel.

Q383: a: Roger Casement. Roger David Casement (previously known as Sir Roger Casement), was an Irish patriot, poet, revolutionary and nationalist by inclination. He was a British diplomat by profession, and is famous for his activities against human rights abuses in the Congo and Peru, but better known for his dealings with Germany prior to Ireland's 1916 Easter Rising. Casement drafted a 'treaty' with Germany that stated Germany's support for an independent Ireland. Most of his time in Germany, however, was spent in an attempt to recruit an 'Irish Brigade' (consisting of Irish prisoners-of-war in the prison camp of Limburg an der Lahn) who would be trained to fight against England.

Casement was arrested in County Kerry on charges of treason, sabotage and espionage against the Crown, three days before the Easter Rising began; and, following a highly publicised trial, stripped of his knighthood and sentenced to death. After an unsuccessful appeal against the death sentence, he was hanged at Pentonville Prison in London on August 3 1916, aged 51.

Q384: b: Running a bomb-making factory. The Maguire Seven case was an infamous miscarriage of justice, in which seven people (including a 14-year-old boy) were imprisoned on the strength of the lies of police officers, lawyers and forensic scientists. On December 3 1973, the Willesden house of Anne Maguire was raided by police and seven people were falsely accused of running a bomb-making factory for the Provisional IRA. They were tried by the Hon Mr Justice Donaldson and, on March 4 1976, all seven were convicted and sentenced to between four and fourteen years imprisonment.

Q385: c: Patrick 'Giuseppe' Conlon. Patrick 'Giuseppe' Conlon, 52, Annie's brother-in-law, received twelve years. Conlon had travelled from Belfast to help his son, Gerard Conlon, who has been falsely accused of the Guildford pub bombing. Giuseppe would die in prison, having had respiratory problems for many years.

Q386: c: 'In The Name of the Father'. 'In the Name of the Father' was a 1993 film, directed by Jim Sheridan and based on the true life story of the Guildford Four (four people falsely convicted of the IRA's Guildford pub bombing, which killed four off-duty British Soldiers and a civilian) and the Maguire Seven (wrongly convicted of running an IRA bomb-making factory). The screenplay was adapted by Terry George and Jim Sheridan from the autobiography, 'Proved Innocent', by Gerry Conlon.

Q387: c: Tony Blair. On February 9 2005, British Prime Minister, Tony Blair, issued a public apology to the Maguire Seven and the Guildford Four for the miscarriages of justice they had suffered. He said: "I am very sorry that they were subject to such an ordeal and such an injustice They deserve to be completely and publicly exonerated".

Q388: a: Judith Ward. Judith Theresa Ward was born January 10 1949. Her unsafe conviction for the Euston Station, National Defence College and M62 coach bombings was quashed on May 11 1992. She had voluntarily confessed due to a mental illness that led to attention-seeking behaviour and the making of false confessions. She spent eighteen years in prison and later wrote a book about her conviction.

Q389: d: 1980. On September 14 1976, newly-convicted prisoner, Kieran Nugent, began the blanket protest in which IRA and Irish National Liberation Army (INLA) prisoners refused to wear prison uniform, and either went naked or wore garments fashioned from prison blankets. In 1978, after a number of attacks on prisoners leaving their cells to 'slop out' (i.e., empty their chamber pots), this escalated into the dirty protest, where prisoners refused to wash and smeared the walls of their cells with excrement. Initially, this protest did not attract a great deal of attention, and even the IRA regarded it as a side-issue and not significant to their armed campaign. It began to attract attention when Tomás Ó Fiaich, the Roman Catholic Archbishop of Armagh, visited the prison and condemned the conditions there. The period leading up to the hunger strike saw a campaign of assassination carried out by both the Irish and British sides. The IRA shot and killed a number of Prison Officers; while loyalist paramilitaries shot and killed a number of activists in the National H-Block/Armagh Committee, badly injuring McAliskey and her husband in an attempt on their lives. On October 27 1980, Republican prisoners in HMP Maze began a hunger strike. Many prisoners volunteered to be part of the strike, but a total of seven were selected to match the number of men who signed the Easter 1916 Proclamation of the Republic.

Q390: b: The right not to wear a prison uniform; the right not to do prison work; the right to free association with other prisoners and to organise educational and recreational pursuits; the right to one visit, one letter and one parcel per week; and full restoration of remission lost through the protest. On October 27 1980, Republican prisoners in HMP Maze began a hunger strike. Many prisoners volunteered to be part of the strike, but a total of seven were selected to match the number of men who signed the Easter 1916 Proclamation of the Republic. The group consisted of IRA members Brendan Hughes, Tommy McKearney, Raymond McCartney, Tom McFeeley, Sean McKenna and Leo Green, and INLA member John Nixon. After a few weeks, three prisoners in Armagh Women's Prison joined the strike, including Mairéad Farrell; and they were followed by a short-lived hunger strike by several dozen more prisoners in HMP Maze. In a war of nerve between the IRA leadership and the British government - with McKenna lapsing in and out of a coma and on the brink of death - the government appeared to concede the essence of the prisoners' five demands with its thirty-page document detailing a proposed settlement. With the document in transit to Belfast, Hughes took the decision to save McKenna's life and end the strike after fifty-three days, on 18 December.

Q391: b: 1981. The second hunger strike took place in 1981 and was a showdown between the prisoners and the British Prime Minister, Margaret Thatcher. One hunger striker, Bobby Sands, was elected as a Member of Parliament during the strike, prompting media interest from around the world.

Q392: c: 10. The strike was called off after ten prisoners had starved themselves to death – including Sands, whose funeral was attended by 100,000 people. The strike radicalised nationalist politics, and was the driving force that enabled Sinn Féin's becoming a mainstream political party.

Q393: a: Internment is the imprisonment or confinement of people (commonly in large groups) without trial.

Q394: c: 1971. Internment began with the arrest of 342 suspected republican guerrillas and paramilitary members on August 9 1971. They were held at HMP Maze. By 1972, 924 men were interned. Serious rioting ensued, and 23 people died in three days. The British government attempted to show some balance by arresting some loyalist paramilitaries later, but out of the 1,981 men interned, only 107 were loyalists.

Q395: d: All of the above. The Belfast Agreement (more commonly known as the Good Friday Agreement or, more rarely, the Stormont Agreement) was a major political development in the Northern Ireland peace process. It was signed in Belfast on April 10 1998 (Good Friday) by the British and Irish governments, and endorsed by most Northern Ireland political parties. It was endorsed by the voters of Northern

Ireland and the Republic of Ireland in separate referendums on May 23 1998. The Democratic Unionist Party was the only large party to oppose the Agreement.

Q396: c: The Maze Prison. The Maze Prison escape (known to Irish Republicans as 'the Great Escape') took place on September 25 1983. Due to the number of prisoners involved, it became known as the biggest prison escape in British history.

Q397: c: 38. A total of 38 Provisional Irish Republican Army (IRA) prisoners escaped from H-Block 7 (H7) of the maximum security Maze Prison (also known as Long Kesh) in County Antrim, Northern Ireland; a prison considered, at the time, one of the most escape-proof in Europe.

Q398: a: 7. During the Troubles, Irish Republican prisoners had escaped from custody en masse on several occasions. On November 17 1971, nine prisoners (dubbed the "Crumlin Kangaroos") escaped from Crumlin Road Jail when rope ladders were thrown over the wall. Two prisoners were recaptured, but the remaining seven managed to cross the border into the Republic of Ireland and appear at a press conference in Dublin. On January 17 1972, seven internees escaped from the prison ship, HMS Maidstone, by swimming to freedom (resulting in their being dubbed the 'Magnificent Seven'). On October 31 1973, three leading IRA members (including former Chief of Staff Seamus Twomey) escaped from Mountjoy Prison in Dublin, when a helicopter landed in the exercise yard of the prison. Irish band, The Wolfe Tones, wrote a song celebrating the escape called 'The Helicopter Song', which topped the Irish music charts. Nineteen IRA members escaped from Portlaoise Jail on August 18 1974, after overpowering guards and using gelignite to blast through the gates. Thirty-three prisoners attempted to escape from Long Kesh on November 6 1974 by digging a tunnel. IRA member, Hugh Coney, was shot dead by a sentry, twenty-nine other prisoners were captured within a few yards of the prison, and the remaining three were back in custody within 24 hours. In March 1975, ten prisoners escaped from the courthouse in Newry, while on trial for attempting to escape from Long Kesh. The escapees included Larry Marley, who would later be one of the masterminds behind the 1983 escape. On June 10 1981, eight IRA members on remand (including Angelo Fusco and Joe Doherty) escaped from Crumlin Road Jail. The men took Prison Officers hostage using three handguns that had been smuggled into the prison, took their uniforms and shot their way out of the prison.

Q399: c: Wormwood Scrubs. In 1979, there was a rooftop protest staged by IRA prisoners over visiting rights. During the rioting, sixty inmates and several Prison Officers were injured. In 1982, an inquiry into the rioting blamed much of the difficulties on failings in the prison management. The prison Governor, John McCarthy, had quit before the rioting, describing Wormwood Scrubs as a "penal dustbin" in a letter to The Times.

Q400: d: 29. Twenty-nine prison staff were killed during the Troubles. Many more suffered violence and intimidation to themselves, their families and property from paramilitaries on both sides.

Q401: b: 3. The Northern Ireland Prison Service currently has three operational establishments:
HMP Maghaberry - A modern, high security prison, housing adult, male, long-term sentenced and remand prisoners in both separated and integrated conditions. Immigration detainees are accommodated in the prison's Belfast facility.
HMP Magilligan - A medium security prison, housing shorter-term, adult, male prisoners, which also has low security accommodation for selected prisoners nearing the end of their sentences.
HM Prison and Young Offenders' Centre, Hydebank Wood - A medium-to-low security establishment, accommodating male young offenders and all female prisoners (including female immigration detainees).
There is also a staff training facility - the Prison Service College - at Millisle, Co Down. The Prison Service Headquarters is located at Dundonald House.

LOCATE THE PRISON

Q402: a: Liverpool. HM Prison Altcourse is a privately-run prison for young offenders and adult male prisoners, located in Fazakerley, near Liverpool, Merseyside. It was built by Tarmac Construction, opened in December 1997, and is operated by GSL Global plc.

Q403: d: Northumberland. HM Prison Acklington is located at Acklington, near Amble, Northumberland, England. It is a category C prison for adult male prisoners. The prison opened in 1972 and has a capacity of 882 inmates. HMP Acklington is the most northerly adult prison in England.

Q404: a: Isle of Wight. HM Prison Albany occupies the site of a former military barracks on the outskirts of Newport on the Isle of Wight, UK. It was designed and built as a Category C Training Prison in the early 1960s. Soon after its opening in 1967, a decision was taken that the security be upgraded and, in 1970, Albany became part of the dispersal system. It suffered major disturbances in 1983, which closed most of the prison for over a year. In 1992, as the result of a major review of the dispersal system, Albany was redesignated as a Category B Closed Training Prison. In January 1998, Albany changed from being half a Vulnerable Prisoner Unit and half a Normal Location, and is now exclusively used for sex offenders and vulnerable prisoners. Albany also operates as an Assessment Centre for the core Sex Offender Treatment Programme.

Q405: d: York. HMP/YOI Askham Grange contributes to the delivery of the Key Objectives of the British Prison Service by delivering a national service to women prisoners (residents) and young offenders, and offers the opportunity for up to ten mothers to maintain full-time care of their children whilst in custody. It is an open prison, which facilitates a comprehensive resettlement regime for long and - increasingly - short-stay residents. Key to the delivery of this regime - and of primary focus to Askham Grange - is the maintenance of decent and respectful relationships between all who live, work and visit here, and the community benefit of pro-social modelling. Support in achieving positive family relationships and learning is provided in parallel with educational and work skills and personal development. Its operational capacity is 131 inmates.

Q406: b: Buckinghamshire. HM Prison Aylesbury Prison (Her Majesty's Young Offender Institution Aylesbury) is in Aylesbury, Buckinghamshire, England. It is situated on the north side of the town centre, on Bierton Road. As a Young Offender Institution, it holds inmates between the ages of 17 and 21 only. The prison is of early Victorian design, and has been on its present site since 1845, following extensive public building in the area that also included the building of the workhouse (now the Tindal Centre). There has been a prison or gaol of some description in Aylesbury since 1180.

Q407: a: Wolverhampton. HMP & YOI Brinsford is a penal establishment in the Wolverhampton area of the English West Midlands. Brinsford holds two categories of prisoner: Juveniles (those aged between 15 and 18) and Young Offenders (those aged over 18). The establishment was opened in 1991 as a YOI and Remand Centre.

Q408: c: Middlesex. HM Prison Bronzefield at Ashford, Middlesex, England, is a purpose-built, privately-run, women's prison. Opened in June 2004 to accommodate 450 women, it includes a mother and baby unit and a special section for women with behavioural problems (the

HDU or High Dependency Unit). HM Prison Bronzefield is the largest female prison in Europe, and is currently the only women's prison to house category A prisoners. (Female and juvenile category a prisoners are called "restricted status" prisoners.) Bronzefield is operated by Kalyx (Sodexho) and staffed by approx 160 Prison Officers (60% of whom are female). The jail has also been the subject of many a news article in the tabloid press, most notably about being too easy a regime for the prisoners and the continued poor industrial relations. There have also been two high profile cases of prisoner-Officer relationships.

Q409: b: Rochdale. HM Prison Buckley Hall is in the Buckley district of Rochdale in Greater Manchester, England. Buckley Hall takes its name from an historic house that previously occupied the site: Buckley Hall.

Q410: d: Essex. Bullwood Hall is in Hockley, Essex, Engand. It was built in the 1960s as a female borstal, and served as a women's prison until 2006, when it was announced that it would become a male prison (due to a shortage of male prison places). Its capacity in 2006 was 184 inmates.

Q411: a: Glasgow. HM Prison Barlinnie is located in the residential suburb of Riddrie, north-east of Glasgow, Scotland, and mainly used for short-term prisoners and those awaiting trial in Glasgow courts, as well as long-term prisoners awaiting transfer to prisons such as Saughton or Peterhead.

Q412: a: Isle of Wight. HM Prison Camp Hill was built in 1912, using prisoner labour from HMP Parkhurst, and opened by Winston Churchill. It lies adjacent to HMP Albany and HMP Parkhurst, on the outskirts of Newport, Isle of Wight, and is a Category C Training Prison.

Q413: b: Rochester. HM Prison Cookham Wood is a closed prison for adult women, near Rochester in Kent, England, with an operational capacity of 140 inmates. It is estimated that more than 40% of the current prison population are captured drug mules, picked up at London's Heathrow and Gatwick airports.

Q414: a: Dundee. Castle Huntly sits approximately seven miles west of Dundee, Scotland. It was built in around 1452 by Baron Gray of Fowlis, under licence from James II of Scotland. In 1947, the castle was refurbished and became a borstal, and then a Young Offenders' Institution, before becoming an open prison for adult male prisoners. It is now known as HMP Castle Huntly, and is one of only two open prisons in Scotland (the other being Noranside Prison). Most prisoners at these establishments are low-risk ones, serving short sentences of less than two years (although some are long sentence prisoners approaching the end of their sentences).

Q415: c: Stirling. Cornton Vale is a women's prison in Stirling, built in 1975, and comprising a total of 217 cells in its 5 houses. It became an women's prison in 1978, under Governor Lady Martha Bruce, and now houses almost all the female adult prisoners and young offenders in Scotland. In April 1999, the compulsory separation of adults and young offenders was legislated; and, in the last two years, a systematic renovation and upgrading of all 5 houses has been carried out.

Q416: a: Sussex. Downview is a closed prison for women in Surrey, England, converted from the former nurses' home of Banstead Hospital. It is located in the borough of Reigate and Banstead, and is immediately adjacent to the southern boundary of Greater London. The prison opened in 1989 as a category C male prison; but, in September 2001, Downview changed it to a closed prison for adult women. The prison holds approximately 50% foreign nationals, many of whom are Jamaican and Nigerian. In December 2004, a sixteen-bed juvenile unit for female offenders aged 15-18 (both remand and convicted) opened in partnership with the Youth Justice Board.

Q417: c: Arundel. HM Prison Ford (informally known as Ford Open Prison) is a low-security prison near Arundel and Littlehampton in West Sussex, England. It is administered by Her Majesty's Prison Service for the Home Office of the United Kingdom government. Ford was formerly a Fleet Air Arm Station, and converted to an open prison in 1960. It has a capacity of around 540, and is renowned for a regime focusing on training and resettlement. The prison houses convicted adult males, and specialises in housing non-violent offenders with a low risk of absconding. It was, until recently, particularly known as the favoured location for the placement of high-profile and celebrity prisoners.

Q418: a: Salford. HM Prison Forest Bank is in Salford, Greater Manchester, England. This is a local prison, holding 1040 adult and young offender males. HMP Forest Bank is a category B prison, although the majority of the inmates are category C. It is a private prison, run by Kalyx (formerly United Kingdom Detention Services (UKDS)) and consists of 6 wings (A-F), a healthcare unit and a segregation unit. The prison holds both remand prisoners from the Wigan and Bolton areas and sentenced prisoners.

Q419: c: Brasside. HM Prison Frankland is a prison located at Brasside,

County Durham, England. It holds male prisoners over the age of 21 whose sentences are more than four years, and high risk remand prisoners. The prison has an operational capacity of 734. It was originally opened in 1980, with four wings, each holding 108 in single cells. A further two wings opened in 1998, to hold an additional 206 inmates. A specialist Dangerous and Severe Personality Disorder Unit opened at the prison in May 2004.

Q420: a: Yorkshire. Full Sutton Prison opened in 1987 as a maximum security prison at Full Sutton near Pocklington, East Yorkshire, England. Full Sutton houses up to 608 prisoners, and is purpose-built for category A and B men. The prison's primary function is to hold in conditions of high security some of the most difficult and dangerous criminals in the country.

Q421: a: Bridgend. HM Prison Parc is in Bridgend, South Wales, and it is run by the private security firm, Securicor. It was the first prison in the UK to be built under the Government's Private Finance Initiative. The prison is very hi-tech, with computer systems, swipe cards and personalised voice identification equipment. The inmates are free to move around certain parts of the prison, using their swipe cards to unlock doors and they can use communal leisure facilities, including a large TV. There is an 8,000 book library, as well as an intensive education and training programme. The inmates earn small amounts of money by doing a variety of jobs in the prison, including low level maintenance work. By using the most up-to-date computer and surveillance equipment, Securicor has cut down the number of staff needed in the prison and increased security, making it more difficult for prisoners to escape.
   The prison used to be a psychiatric hospital, until it was closed down and patients moved to either other hospitals in the area or into the community. The prison has a capacity of 1000 inmates and is classed as a category B prison.

Q422: c: Leicester. HMYOI & RC Glen Parva was constructed in the early 1970s as a borstal, and has always held young offenders. Since its opening in 1974, the establishment has seen considerable expansion and change, and now serves a catchment area of over 100 courts, holding a mixture of sentenced, unsentenced and remand prisoners.

Q423: a: Uttoxeter. HM prison Dovegate is a class B, adult male prison, near Uttoxeter, Staffordshire, England.

Q424: b: Suffolk. Hollesley Bay is located near Woodbridge in the county of Suffolk in England, and is used to house category D prisoners. Hollesley Bay began in 1887 as a colonial college, training those intending to emigrate. In 1938, the Prison Commission purchased the site for use as a Borstal, and it became a Young Offenders Institution in 1988, when Youth Custody replaced the borstal system. With the opening of Warren Hill in 2002, Hollesley Bay became for the sole use of adult offenders.

Hollesley Bay has the largest prison farm in the British Prison System.

Q425: b: North Yorkshire. HM Prison Kirklevington Grange is located at Yarm in North Yorkshire, England. The prison opened in 1992 as a Resettlement Prison for category C and D adult male offenders nearing the end of their sentences and intending to settle in the north-east of England. The prison has an operational capacity of 223, and was originally constructed in 1965 as a mixed remand centre.

Q426: c: Doncaster. Lindholme Prison, situated on Lindholme Moor in the Metropolitan Borough of Doncaster, South Yorkshire, England, is a split site comprising a category C medium security prison and an Immigration Removal Centre.

Q427: d: Evesham. HM Prison Long Lartin is situated in Evesham, Worcestershire, England. The capacity of the prison is 492 and it houses prisoners with a minimum sentence of four years, category A and B prisoners, as well as category A remand prisoners. In 1971, Long Lartin Prison was officially opened as a Category C Training Prison. However, in 1972, additional security features and systems were added to enable it to operate as a Dispersal Prison.

Q428: b: Brasside. HM Prison Low Newton is a prison and Young Offenders Institution located at Brasside, County Durham,, England. Since 1998, HMP Low Newton has been an all-female jail, taking female remand prisoners from across the north of England, as well as lifers and juveniles. It has an operational capacity of 396 (as of February 2004). The prison was originally constructed in 1965 as a mixed remand centre.

Q429: a: Hertfordshire. The Mount Prison opened in 1987 as a Young Offenders Institution. It was designed as a Category C Training Prison, built on the site of a former RAF station on the outskirts of Bovingdon village, Hertfordshire. The prison regime includes full/part-time education, workshops, training courses, farms and gardens and a works department. Various types of offending behaviour groups are available, eg. drug group (suppliers), drug group (users), anger management and alcohol offending. Other special features include: listener groups (community based project to keep juveniles out of prison), a job skills course and prisoner-driven drug-free meetings.

Q430: c: Lincolnshire. HMP North Sea Camp is an open prison near Boston, Lincolnshire, England. It opened as a Borstal in 1935, having been established by a group of Borstal Trainees who had been marched cross-country from Stafford. They set up a campsite and immediately began work, building a sea wall to protect the site from the North Sea. Once this was complete, they began reclaiming land by building a further sea wall - that land then became the prison farm. Until the sale of adjacent land in 2004, the prison had the biggest prison farm in the United Kingdom, much of which was on land reclaimed from the The Wash. Today, North Sea Camp is an adult male prison, holding 306 prisoners. In August 2006 Activities included prison education, workshops and a laundry, and a number of prisoners worked outside the prison on day-release. The prison also has a small terrace of self-contained houses for life sentence prisoners who are coming close to parole.

Q431: c: Yorkshire. Northallerton is the former county gaol for the North Riding of Yorkshire. The establishment dates from 1783 and has had a number of changes of role over the years, including use as a military prison, a Training Prison for adults and a remand centre. Since the summer of 2002, it has operated as a Young Offender Institution for prisoners serving less than two years.

Q432: b: Rugby. Onley Prison is situated in Rugby, Warwickshire in the Midlands of England. Opened as a Borstal in 1968, Onley became a Young Offender Prison in 1976. Onley is a category C establishment, accepting all suitable determinate sentence prisoners. It began housing prisoners over the age of 18 in February 2003.

Q433: a: Isle of Wight. HM Prison Parkhurst is situated in Parkhurst, Isle of Wight. Parkhurst (or Central Prison, as it is officially known) is one of three closely associated prisons; the other two being Camp Hill and Albany. Parkhurst and Albany were once amongst the few top security prisons in the United Kingdom, but were downgraded in the 1990s. Parkhurst enjoyed notoriety as one of the toughest jails in the British Isles; and many notable felons, including the Richardson brothers and the Kray twins, were incarcerated there.

Q434: a: Surrey. HM Prison Send is a women's prison in Send, near Woking in Surrey, United Kingdom. The site was originally an isolation hospital, and became junior detention centre in 1962. In 1987, it became a Category C Training Prison for adult males. It was rebuilt in 1999 and is now a closed female Training Prison. It has a capacity of 218 prisoners. Famous inmates include Jane Andrews, a friend of the Duchess of York serving life for killing her boyfriend, Thomas Cressman.

Q435: b: Rutland. HM Prison Stocken is a Category C Closed Training Prison in Stretton, in the county of Rutland. Built in 1985 as a Young Offender Institution, HMP Stocken has since expanded, with new wings added in 1990, 1997, 1998 and a MTU opened in April 2003.

Q436: c: Cheshire. Styal Prison is a women's prison in Wilmslow, Cheshire, United Kingdom, built as an ophanage in the 1890s. In 1956, this closed and the site re-opened as a women's prison in 1962, with women transferred from HMP Strangeways. It holds 459 prisoners, 80% of whom arrive with multiple drug problems.

Q437: a: Cheshire. Thorn Cross is a purpose-built, open Young Offender Institution, situated near Warrington in Cheshire. It opened in 1985 on the site of a former Royal Naval Air Station, which was initially used as an open adult establishment. The regime includes provision of farms and gardens and training courses, Parentcraft, drug awareness, anger management, car crime, Fire Cadets and SDP. There are also Offending Behaviour Programmes, Resettlement Programme for job/training placement and mentoring. Thorn Cross has a number of partnerships with national and local employers.

Q438: c: Dorset. The Verne is one of HM Prisons on Tophill, on the Isle of Portland in Dorset, England. It occupies a former Army Citadel, built by convicts in the 19th Century to protect Portland Port and Portland Harbour. It is particularly used for prisoners who are foreign nationals.

Q439: a: Norfolk. Wayland Prison is in the county of Norfolk, England, and located near the village of Griston. The prison opened in 1985, and is used for category C inmates. As of October 2006, the prison had a capacity of 709 inmates in its eight residential units. Most cells are single occupancy, though the Induction Wing (and some selected cells in the main wings) are shared. Two of the accommodation units are designated for those taking part in Sex Offender Treatment Programmes. The prison has been enlarged on three occasions.

Q440: d: West Yorkshire. On April 1 1995, HM Prisons Thorp Arch and Rudgate amalgamated to form HMP Wealstun in the Wetherby area of West Yorkshire. The amalgamation of two neighbouring establishments was an historic development for the Prison Service, and had the effect of creating a category C (closed) side and category D (open) side within one establishment. A central tenet of Wealstun's whole establishment approach was to enable the progressive transfer of suitable prisoners from the closed side to the open side. The utilisation of joint services enables Wealstun to make financial savings whilst maintaining the good reputation of both establishments. A great deal of building development has taken place and some continues.

Q441: c: Kent. HMP Elmley is situated on the Isle of Sheppey in Kent. Elmley is a purpose-built local prison, serving all courts in the county of Kent. The establishment opened in 1992, and includes a category C unit for 240 prisoners built in 1997, and a Vulnerable Prisoner Unit delivering the Sex Offender Treatment Programme. In addition, there is also a Drug Rehabilitation Unit and Detox Programme.

Q442: b: Portland. In 1997, the UK established the Weare as a temporary measure to ease prison overcrowding. Weare was docked at the disused Royal Navy dockyard at the Isle of Portland. On March 9 2005, it was announced that Weare was to close, mainly due to the costly running and its being unnecessary. Among the options of what to do with the ship were moving it to London - and sinking it in Portland Harbour or around the Isle of Portland as a man-made reef and diving location.

Q443: d: Cambridgeshire. HM Prison Whitemoor is near the town of March in Cambridgeshire, England. Built in an old railway marshalling yard, Whitemoor is a maximum security prison for men, first opened in 1992, housing around 500 of the most dangerous prisoners in the UK. The prison houses a Dangerous Severe Personality Disorder (DSPD) unit and a Close Supervision Centre (CSC). HMP Whitemoor does not accept any prisoners who are serving less than four years.

Q444: a: Yorkshire. HMP Wolds is located south-west of Everthorpe, East Riding of Yorkshire, England. It opened in April 1992 as a remand prison; and, in 1993, became a local category B prison, holding sentenced prisoners. It was the first private prison to be opened in the United Kingdom. Wolds Prison is now for mid-term category C prisoners (including second stage lifers).

Q445: d: Isle of Sheppey. Standford Hill is on the site of an old Royal Air Force station. The prison was first used in 1950, but the current accommodation was built in 1986. The prison holds category D sentenced male adults.

Q446: b: Milton Keynes. HMP Woodhill is a category A (high security) prison on the western edge of Milton Keynes, England, with a remand unit for local magistrate court use. This prison first opened in July 1992, and was extended in 1996. In 2001, a Protected Witness Unit was added. There is also a Young Offenders Unit on an adjacent site.

Q447: a: West London. Wormwood Scrubs is a category B local prison (i.e. an establishment that receives prisoners from the courts, either on remand or after sentencing). It is located on the south of Wormwood Scrubs, in the London borough of Hammersmith and Fulham. It was built in the 1880s, using prison labour; and until 1902, it housed both male and female prisoners. It currently has accommodation for 1256 prisoners in five wings.

Q448: b: Thamesmead. Belmarsh became operational on April 2 1991, and is a local prison, serving primarily the Central Criminal Court and magistrates Courts in South East London. In addition, the establishment serves Crown and Magistrates Courts in South West Essex. Belmarsh also holds category A prisoners.

Q449: c: Isle of Sheppey. Swaleside is a Category B Training Prison, with 775 prisoners, more than half of whom are serving life sentences.

Q450: d: North London. HM Prison Pentonville was built in 1842, in North London. Its design was influenced by the 'separate system' developed at Eastern State Penitentiary in Philadelphia, and was amongst the first of the UK's modern prisons. It had separate cells for 860 prisoners, and proved satisfactory - to the authorities at least; thus commencing a programme of prison building to deal with the rapid increase in prisoner numbers (occasioned by the ending of capital punishment for many crimes and a steady reduction in the use of transportation).

A- Z INDEX OF PRISON - AND CRIME-RELATED WORDS AND PHRASES

A

Absolute discharge: The court takes no further action against the offender, but the offence and discharge will remain on his criminal record.

Acquisitive crime: Offences by which the offender derives material gain.

Acquittal: An acquittal is where, at the end of a trial, the court finds the suspect not guilty.

Aggravated offence: [*Please see 'Racially or religiously aggravated offence'.*]

Amnesty: An amnesty is the police request for people to hand in illegal goods (usu. weapons), in the knowledge that those in possession will not be charged or prosecuted.

Anti-Social Behaviour Order (ASBO): An Anti-Social Behaviour Order is a civil order banning the subject from entering certain areas, associating with certain people or doing certain things.

Appeal court: The appeal court is the higher court to which cases are sent when either the defence or prosecution (if it is an appeal about the sentence) wish to challenge the result of a Magistrates or Crown Court case.

Arrest: An arrest is where one suspected of an offence is lawfully detained by a constable.

Association: Association is the name given to prisoners' leisure time spent outside of their cells.

Asylum seeker: An asylum seeker is a person seeking to be declared a refugee and live in another country, after fleeing their home country due to the conditions there.

B

Bail remand: A suspect who has been arrested and charged with an offence is released by the police or court on the condition that they report back at a certain date and time. Sometimes the suspect also has to keep to certain other conditions, such as living in a particular place or not going near witnesses.

Barrister: A barrister is a lawyer who has been called to the bar and is qualified to appear in all courts.

British Crime Survey (BCS): The British Crime Survery is the annual Home Office survey of people's experience of crime and their feelings about crime, covering England and Wales

C

Canteen: The canteen is the prison shop where inmates can purchase a limited range of goods using their pay or private cash sent in by family and friends.

Caution: A caution is the official warning given to offenders who admit their guilt.

The Criminal Injuries Compensation Authority: The Criminal Injuries Compensation Authority is the government agency that pays damages to victims of violent crimes and those injured trying to apprehend criminals or prevent a crime.

Community Order: A Community Order is a court sentence to

be served in the community. As part of the Community Order, the court may order the offender to fulfil a number of requirements; including drug or alcohol treatment and testing, electronic monitoring (tagging), curfew, living at a specified address, unpaid work, doing or refraining from doing certain things or entering certain places and attending certain offending behaviour programmes. The new Community Order came into effect in April 2005.

Compensation: Compensation is the money paid by the offender to compensate the victim for the physical or psychological damage caused by the offence.

Concurrent sentence: A concurrent sentence refers to two or more sentences to be served at the same time; eg. 'a three year and a four year sentence to run concurrently' amounts to a four year sentence, as the first three years of both were served at the same time. [Opposite to 'Consecutive sentence'.]

Conditional discharge: A conditional discharge means no further action is to be taken against the offender unless they commit a further offence within a given period (no more than 3 years).

Consecutive sentence: A consecutive sentence is where two or more sentences are to run one after the other and are usually custodial; eg. 'two sentences of three years to run consecutively' amounts to a six year sentence. [Opposite to 'Concurrent sentence'.]

Conviction: When an offender has pleaded - or been found - guilty of an offence in a court, s/he is said to have been convicted. The conviction then appears on the offender's criminal record.

Criminal Cases Review Commission: Public body responsible for investigating alleged miscarriages of justice.

Criminal responsibility: The age of criminal responsibility is the age at which a young person is held legally responsible for their own behaviour and can be found guilty in a court.

Cross-examination: Cross-examination is where a witness in a court case is questioned about their evidence by the solicitor or barrister representing the opposing side; so a prosecution witness is cross-examined by a defendent's lawyer, and a defence witness by a prosecution lawyer

Crown Court: The Crown Court is the second tier in the English court system. A Judge hears the cases, and trials are heard by a jury. The Crown Court deals with crime that is too serious to be heard by the magistrates' court, as well as cases referred by the magistrates for sentence because their sentencing powers are not adequate.

Crown Prosecution Service (CPS): The Crown Prosecution Service is the public prosecution service. The Crown Prosecution Service decides whether there is enough evidence to take a case to court, and whether it would be in the public interest to do so. After the decision to prosecute has been taken, the CPS employs the lawyers to represent the prosecution at court.

Curfew Order (tagging): The Court can order an offender to be at home between certain hours. This is usually monitored using an electronic tag attached to the offender's ankle.

Custodial sentences: Custodial sentences are those that involve the offender being locked up in a prison, young offender institution or secure training centre.

D

Defendent: The defendent is the person accused of a crime in court.

Detention and training order: A detention and training order is the mechanism by which a youth court sentences children aged 12-17 years to a custodial sentence.

Discharge absolute, conditional discharge: When the offender is found guilty of the offence, the conviction will appear on his or her criminal record; but, either no further action is taken at all (absolute discharge), or no further action is taken as long as the offender does not offend again in a certain period of time (conditional discharge).

Dispersal Prison: High security prison. There are a number of high security prisons and they are used to disperse around the country the prisoners in need of the highest levels of security, rather than keeping them all in one place.

DNA: DNA is deoxyribonucleic acid. These are the molecules contained in all living matter that possess unique identification information. Everyone's DNA is slightly different, so DNA found in body cells at crime scenes is increasingly being used as evidence in court.

Drug mule: A drug mule is a person (usually a young female) who acts as a courier for illegal drugs.

Drug Treatment and Testing Order: A Drug Treatment and Testing Order is a sentence for drug users that consists of receiving treatment for drug use and giving regular urine samples to prove they are no longer using drugs.

Due process: The guidelines for criminal cases that seek to ensure a fair trial.

E

Electronic tagging: An offender on bail, a curfew order or Home Detention Curfew at the end of their prison sentence has an electronic tag that alerts staff in a control centre if

they leave the house during the parts of the day when they
have been ordered to stay at home.

F

Fine: A fine is a sentence that involves the offender paying
money to the court as a punishment. If the fine is too big to
be paid immediately, the offender can usually pay it in
weekly or monthly instalments over a period of months (up to
a year).

Fixed penalty notice: A fixed penalty notice is an on-the-spot
fine of up to £80 that can be given to any person over the age
of 16 for engaging in certain types of criminal or 'antisocial'
behaviour.

Forensic Science Service: The Forensic Science Service is a
government owned company that supplies forensic science
services to police forces in England and Wales.

G

Grievous Bodily Harm (GBH): Grievous Bodily Harm is
serious injury inflicted by one person on another.

H

Hate crime: A hate crime committed against a person
because of the offender's irrational hatred of one of the
victim's characteristics; usually their race, religion, a physical
or learning disability, gender or sexual orientation.

Her Majesty's Inspectorate of Prisons: Her Majesty's
Inspectorate of Prisons was established in 1980 to inspect
prisons working independently of the Prison Service and
reporting directly to the Home Secretary.

Heroin, smack, junk, brown, H: Heroin is a highly addictive

opiate, usually consumed by smoking, injecting or snorting through the nose.

Home Detention Curfew (tagging): A prisoner serving a sentence of between 8 months and 4 years can be released up to 90 days early under strict curfew arrangements that involve wearing an electronic tag.

Home Office: Home Office is the government department responsible for all national crime and security issues, such as policing and immigration.

I

Independent Monitoring Board: The Independent Monitoring Board are the committees of volunteers appointed by the Home Secretary to monitor prison conditions and the treatment of prisoners. Every prison has an Independent Monitoring Board.

Indictable offence: An indictable offence is a serious offence that can only be dealt with in the Crown Court.

Institutionalised: When someone has been in an institution (such as a prison) for a long period of time, they may lose the ability to cope with aspects of normal day-to-day life because they are not used to making decisions for themselves. They are then described as institutionalised.

Intensive Supervision and Surveillance programme: Intensive Supervision and Surveillance programmes are the most rigorous non-custodial intervention for persistent young offenders, combining community-based surveillance with up to 25 hours of contact time per week.

J

Judge: A Judge is the person who presides over the higher

criminal courts (the Crown Court and Court of Appeal). Judges are trained lawyers who have been appointed after distinguished careers as barristers or solicitors.

K

Kerb crawling: 'Kerb crawling' is when someone drives slowly along the kerb seeking sex from prostitutes.

L

Lawyer: 'Lawyer' is the generic term used to describe barristers (who usually work in the Crown Court and Appeal Court) and solicitors.

Legislation: 'Legislation' is a general term for the Acts of Parliament that make up the laws of the land.

On licence: The period of time between the end of a custodial sentence and the end of the entire sentence, during which the sentenced person is released into the community (usually under certain conditions) is known as being 'on licence'.

Local Authority Secure Children's Home: Local Authority Children's Homes are establishments for the housing of children aged 12-14 and 'vulnerable' boys aged 15 and 16. They are usually small in size, with between five and thirty-eight beds.

Local prison: A 'local prison' is one used for prisoners on remand who are newly sentenced. Local prisons tend to be near to the courts, and often situated in towns and cities. Once they have been sentenced, most prisoners are moved to training prisons to serve their sentences.

M

Magistrate: A magistrate is one who sits as part of a group of three and acts as a Judge in the magistrates court. Magistrates in England and Wales are volunteers who have been specially trained for the task, and receive no payment other than their expenses.

Magistrates court: The magistrates court deals with most motoring offences and less serious crime. The Judges in the magistrates court are either a group of three lay (volunteer) magistrates or a District Judge (who is a professional). The magistrates court has limits on sentencing powers, and can send cases to the Crown Court for sentence where necessary.

Miscarriage of justice: A miscarriage of justice is a conviction shown to be unsafe by new evidence in the case or evidence of an unfair trial or violation of the rights of the accused.

Mother and Baby Unit: A designated separate living accommodation within a women's prison that enables imprisoned mothers to have their children with them (up to the age of 9 or 18 months).

N

No further action: 'No further action' is the official terminology to describe the police's decision not to pursue the offence/offender and to drop all charges.

Notifiable offence: A notifiable offence is one deemed serious enough to be recorded by the Police. This includes most indictable and triable-either-way offences.

O

Offender: An offender is one who has been convicted of a crime.

Offending Behaviour Programme: An Offending Behaviour Programme is a programme of work undertaken by an offender that is designed to tackle the reasons or behaviour which led to his/her offending. These programmes often involve work with groups of offenders, but some are one-to one. Many of them are based on cognitive behavioural therapy and are accredited by a national accreditation board. Offending behaviour programmes currently available in prison and through the probation service include the Enhanced Thinking Skills programme (ETS), the Sex Offender Treatment Programme and The Drink Impaired Drivers Programme.

Open prison: An open prison is one with minimum security requirements, and houses those offenders who are deemed not to pose a threat to the general public.

P

Perpetrator: [See 'Offender'.]

Police-recorded crime: Police-recorded crime is a method of compiling crime statistics based on a number - but not all - crimes reported to the police. Recorded crime figures tend to be significantly lower than actual crime rates.

Probation Community Order: Although people still talk of offenders 'getting probation', what that now means is that the offender receives a Community Order. The Community Order may include any number of the thirteen requirements: drug or alcohol treatment and testing, electronic monitoring (tagging), curfew, living at a specified address, unpaid work, doing or refraining from doing certain things or entering certain places, attending certain Offending Behaviour Programmes. An offender is considered to have breached a Community Order if they fail to comply with a requirement or commit another offence while the order is still in force. Courts may then impose more requirements or send the offender to prison.

Prosecution: 'Prosecution' refers the case brought against a person, and the lawyer(s) responsible for putting forward the case against a defendent.

Q

Queen's Counsel ('King's Counsel' when the monarch is male): A Queen's Counsel (QC) is a barrister appointed counsel to the Crown, due to their seniority and merit. They are also known as 'a silk' due to the silk gown they wear.

Queen's evidence: 'Queen's evidence' refers to evidence given for the prosecution by an accomplice against his former criminal associates (e.g. "Turn queen's evidence").

R

Racially- or **religiously-aggravated offence:** Racially- and religiously-motivated offences are defined in section 28 of the Crime and Disorder Act of 1998. An offence is considered more serious (and carries a higher sentence) when motivated by racist or religious hostility.

Re-offend recidivism: Re-offend recidivism is where an offender commits a new crime after being convicted of a previous offence.

Reasonable doubt: The standard of proof in UK criminal courts is that the case is proved 'beyond reasonable doubt'.

Recidivism re-offending: The rate of recidivism is the rate of reoffending; for example, "the rate of recidivism for prisoners is 58%".

Refugee: A refugee is an asylum seeker who has met the terms set out under the 1951 UN Convention on the Status of Refugees.

Rehabilitation: 'Rehabilitation' is the work given to offenders to enable them to leave their 'life of crime'. This often involves tackling the specific reasons for the offending (e.g. drug use, lack of understanding of victims' feelings), as well as dealing with other factors that are known to help people lead crime free lives (education/ basic skills, housing, employment, parenting skills).

Remand in custody: Remanding in custody is where a defendent is imprisoned while awaiting trial.

Repeat victimisation: Repeat victimisation is where certain people and/or places suffer repeated incidences of crime.

Resettlement: The reintegration and re-housing of an offender after release from custody is known as 'resettlement'.

Restorative justice: Restorative justice is an approach that aids the offender in seeking to put right the harm caused by their offence. This may involve a meeting between the offender and victim (with a mediator), where the victim tells the offender how the offence has affected them, and the offender can attempt to put things right.

S

Section 90/91 of the Powers of Criminal Courts (Sentencing) Act (2000): This gives the Crown Court the power to sentence children aged 10-17 to prison for serious offences (for which an adult would receive a sentence of 14 years or more).

Secure training centre (STC): A secure training centre is an institution for 12-14 year olds. Children in this age group who are persistent offenders or who have committed a serious offence are not sent to prison, but to an STC.

Self-harm: Self-harm is where people deliberately hurt or

injure themselves, often in response to extreme stress, depression or a particularly difficult situation.

Soliciting: Soliciting is approaching or confronting someone with an offer of sexual services in return for payment.

Solicitor: A solicitor is a lawyer who advises clients on matters of law, prepares cases, and may only appear in certain courts.

Statement: A statement is a description of the events of a crime - or information relating to a crime - that is given to the police during an investigation.

Summary offence: A summary offence is one considered to be less serious, and dealt with only in the magistrates court.

Suspect: A suspect is a person investigated in relation to a particular offence or offences.

T

Tagging, electronic monitoring: An offender on bail, curfew order or Home Detention Curfew at the end of a prison sentence has an electronic tag that alerts staff in a control centre if the offender leaves their house during the parts of the day in which they have been ordered to stay at home.

Training Prison: A Training Prison is one to which convicted prisoners are sent to serve their sentences. Training courses and education are usually made available to prisoners there long enough to benefit from them.

V

Verdict: The verdict in a criminal trial is the point at which the magistrates (in a magistrates court) or the jury (in the Crown

Court) say whether they have found the defendant guilty or not guilty.

Victimisation, being a victim: The term 'victimisation' is usually used to describe the risk of becoming a victim of crime; for example, those belonging to a particular group (women, children, ethnic minorities, inhabitants of a particular area, etc.), or those connected with repeat victimisation (someone who has already been a victim is victimised again).

Victimology: Victimology is the study of victims and the factors relating to being a crime victim.

Visitors' centre: A visitors' centre is a place, usually outside a prison, where people visiting imprisoned relatives or friends can obtain information, help and refreshments, and wait for their visits. (Not all prisons have visitors' centres.)

W

White-collar crime: 'White-collar crime' is the term usually used to describe those crimes committed by professional people, often in relation to business or financial affairs. Examples include corrupt share transactions, tax evasion and fraud.

Y

Young Offender Institution: A Young Offender Institution is a prison for young people between the ages of 15 or 16 (16 for girls) and 21. Young offenders have to be kept separate from adults, and juveniles (those under 18) from those aged 18-21.

Youth Justice Board: The Youth Justice Board is an executive, non-departmental public body, responsible for overseeing the Youth Justice System.

Youth Offending Team (YOT): There is a YOT in every local authority in England and Wales, and they are made up of representatives from the police, the Probation Service, social services, Health, Education, Drugs and Alcohol Misuse and Housing Officers. The YOT is responsible for coordinating the work of the Youth Justice Services.

Z

Zero tolerance: 'Zero tolerance' is a crime-fighting strategy developed in New York in the 1990s, where all crimes - however minor - and forms of antisocial behaviour are dealt with rigorously in order to combat a supposed 'culture of crime'.

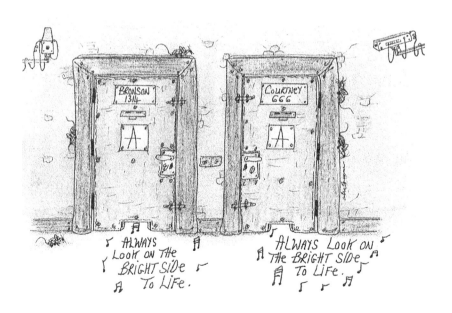

NOTES:

NOTES:

REVIEWS:

"This book is yet another winner from Apex Publishing Ltd. Written by two men who, between them, though from different sides of the screw/con divide, have a lot more knowledge about the prison system than a herd of Home Secretaries. An entertaining and informative addition to the British prison experience genre, and unique in the amount of important information the authors manage to impart about both the history of prison and the mechanics of contemporary incarceration in this country. Featuring plenty of examples of Dave Courtney's trademark wit along with Jim Dawkins' qualified perspective on the organisation he was once a part of before coming to his senses.
The British Crime and Prison Quiz Book more than lives up to it's title, and should be required reading fro every hobbit in the Home Office and Prison Service HQ, maybe it would give them half a clue about the system they are supposed to be running. But for the rest of us it's just a cracking book, a guided tour through the wings and along the landings of our jails with a couple of tour guides who really know their stuff. And with a foreword by Charlie Bronson, how can it miss? Buy it, read it, test your cellmate!"
- Noel 'Razor' Smith, Author of 'Warrior Kings'

"A law-dodging, prison-breaking riot of a quiz that's perfect for those who might have a lot of 'time' on their hands."
- Jeff Maysh, Loaded Magazine

"From two oracles of the true crime genre, with hundreds of astonishing facts on the criminal and prison world, this impeccably researched and flawlessly put together book will have you enthralled, captivated and laughing out loud!"
- Robin Barratt, Bodyguards and Bouncers Magazine (Editor)

REVIEWS:

"A classic combination of 'two' top authors in their own right. Dave Courtney renowned to bring a few smiles with his wit and charm. Jim Dawkins renowned to raise a few eyebrows with his truthfulness and sincerity. This is CRIME & PUNISHMENT united in this unusual book of trivia. Only the genius of Chris Cowlin of Apex Publishing Ltd could forge together such authors in a fun packed book leaving many thinking, "I didn't know that". An excellent book, a test of knowledge on crime and the prison system. 10 out of 10 ... "

- Leighton Frayne, Author of 'The Frayne Bros'

"This book is an absolute gem. To be honest, when I first looked at the manuscript I honestly thought it would be over-burdened with questions such as, "Who cut so-and-so's left ear off in Putney in 1963?" Not a chance. Dawkins and Courtney have put together an absolute blinder that covers everything from the finer points of Roman law to Anglo Saxon criminal justice, and the sections dealing with prison regulations are a true eye-opener.
Truth to tell, I HATE reading quiz books, although writing them and reviewing them are different kettles of fish. This volume is one I can honestly say it has been a pleasure to peruse.
Dawkins and Courtney both have an expert insight into the world of crime, although for radically different reasons. They obviously have an incredible rapport with each other when it comes to writing, for their partnership has produced a fact-filled volume that one will never tire of reading.
Trust me, you really WILL enjoy reading the Crime Quiz Book. By the time you get to the end, you'll probably have forgotten more about Crime than Dixon of Dock Green or Reagan from The Sweeney ever knew! Absolute magic."

- Mike Hallowell, The Shields Gazette

"An excellent duo of authors for a quiz book on crime and prison, brilliantly written and brilliantly put together."

- Lindsay Frayne, Author of 'The Frayne Bros'

REVIEWS:

"This book is full of surprises, it shocks, it twists, it takes you in and out of the underworld and into the nick, it's unpredictable ...
IT'S A 100% WINNER!"
- **Tel Currie, Author of 'Heroes and Villains'**

"An ex-screw and renowned convict coming together for a book may seem like a match made in hell – which is not far off the truth according to the goings on within HM Belmarsh exposed in Jim Dawkins's excellent book The Loose Screw – but this is a heavenly collection of Q&A's with a difference.
Loveable rogue Dave Courtney has teamed up with Dawkins to produce what can only be described as one of the most unique collection of brain teasers that goes much further than a conventional quiz book. There are questions in here on Her Majesty's prison service that will have Queen Liz herself scratching her head with her quill.
Much more than a quiz book I say because every answer is backed up with facts and statements so by the time you are done ... you can be the font of all knowledge down your local boozer ... or the prison exercise yard!
Superb work by two great fellas that have experienced both sides of the 'iron bar' divide."
- **David Williams, Author of 'Desert England'**

An incredible amount of research has gone into this – an excellent book which I will read again and again.
- **Jason Marriner, Author of 'It's Only A Game'**